BEHIND THE GUNS

The History of Battery I, 2ⁿᵈ Regiment

Illinois Light Artillery

Shawnee Classics

A Series of Classic Regional Reprints for the Midwest

Edited with a Foreword by CLYDE C. WALTON

Preface by W. G. PUTNEY

BEHIND THE GUNS

The History of **BATTERY I**

2nd Regiment, Illinois Light Artillery

THADDEUS C. S. BROWN

SAMUEL J. MURPHY

WILLIAM G. PUTNEY

SOUTHERN ILLINOIS UNIVERSITY PRESS

CARBONDALE AND EDWARDSVILLE

Library of Congress Cataloging-in-Publication Data

Brown, Thaddeus C. S., 1838–1927.
    Behind the guns : the history of Battery I, 2nd Regiment, Illinois Light Artillery /
Thaddeus C. S. Brown, Samuel J. Murphy, William G. Putney.
        p. cm.
    Includes bibliographical references and index.
    1. United States. Army. Illinois Light Artillery Regiment, 2nd. Battery I (1861–1865)
2. Illinois—History—Civil War, 1861–1865—Regimental histories. 3. United
States—History—Civil War, 1861–1865—Regimental histories. 4. United
States—History—Civil War, 1861–1865—Artillery operations. I. Murphy, Samuel J.,
1834–1918. II. Putney, William G., 1842–1919. III. Title.

E505.8 2nd .B76 2000
973.7'473—dc21
ISBN 0-8093-2342-7 (alk. paper)   00-029164

The illustrations in this volume are from contemporary sources. Mr. Andor Braun designed
the typography and format.

The paper used in this publication meets the minimum requirements of American National
Standard for Information Sciences—Permanence of Paper for Printed Library Materials,
ANSI Z39.48-1992. ⊚

CONTENTS

LIST OF MAPS

FOREWORD

by Clyde C. Walton

WHETHER the experiences of the men of Battery I, 2nd Illinois Light Artillery, were similar to the experiences of members of other artillery units is not certain. Much attention has been paid to the foot soldiers of the infantry units and to the men who rode to war with the cavalry, but not much attention has been centered on field artillery units. Many more men served in the infantry and cavalry than in the artillery; for example, Illinois furnished to the Union army 152 infantry regiments, 17 cavalry regiments, but only 33 batteries of artillery. There are 299 memoirs, reminiscences, and histories of Illinois infantry units, 68 of cavalry, but only 20 of artillery units. Much of what is in print about Illinois artillery is fragmentary and often little more than a chronology.

The surviving manuscript records of Battery I in the Illinois State Archives in Springfield, are incomplete and occasionally do not agree with the brief published record of the Battery issued by the Illinois Adjutant General after the close of the war. Even so, it is possible to sketch in the outlines of the history of the Battery, from its first members to its final muster out. Some details of the battery's history remain obscure, and there is a curious lack of biographical details of its members—as a small example, almost nothing is known of one of the battery's original officers, Junior 2nd Lieutenant William Eugene Hayward. But if some aspects of battery activity are unknown, the details of its organization and action at the front constitute a verified record of patriotic service.

In the summer and fall of 1861 a number of men had been given authority either by the governor or by the War Department, to raise troops in Illinois. At this time in the war, authority was frequently given to men who thought they could recruit a regiment or a company or a battery; later the raising of troops would be handled entirely by the governor and would become more formalized and more routine. Battery I would be formed from soldiers enlisted by two men—Charles W. Keith of Joliet, Illinois, and Henry B. Plant of Peoria, Illinois.

Keith went to work to sign up men for a unit to be called the "Joliet Light Artillery," and inserted the following notices on September 24, 1861, in the local newspaper, the *Joliet Signal:*

JOLIET LIGHT ARTILLERY.—By notice in another column, it will be seen that Capt. C. W. Keith has been authorized to raise a company of Light Artillery. This is the most desirable branch of the service; and those of our brave young men who wish to take a hand in the fight for the Union and the constitution, should enlist in Captain Keith's company. We learn that the company is designed for the Western frontier.

JOLIET LIGHT ARTILLERY CO.

I am now authorized to enlist a company for the Artillery service. PAY AND SUBSISTANCE FROM DATE OF ENLISTMENT. FAMILIES OF VOLUNTEERS PROVIDED FOR.

All active and reliable men wishing to enter this arm of the service will do well to call at the recruiting office (in Bushe's new building opposite National Hotel,) without delay as the company will not be long in filling up.

Full Battery Company—Captain, 4 Lieutenants, 8 Sargents, 12 Corporals, 2 Buglers, 125 Privates, 110 Horses and 4 Guns. Men armed with Revolvers and Sabers. No army in the world receives as good fare and pay as Uncle Sam's.

CHAS. W. KEATH [sic], *Capt.*

His first recruits (including himself) signed the roll on October 1. These first 29 men included 23 from Joliet who enlisted in Joliet; 1 from Joliet and 2 from Plainfield, these 3 enlisting in Plainfield, some nine miles northwest of Joliet; 2 more from Channahon, enlisting in that town some eight miles southwest of Joliet; and 1 from Bloomington, enlisting in Bloomington which is about one hundred miles from Joliet. These 29 men from four communities form the nucleus of Battery I. But although Keith could conceivably have signed men in Joliet, Plainfield, and Channahon on the same day, he could hardly have enlisted men in these three cities and in Bloomington, one hundred miles away, on the same day.

The muster rolls in the Illinois State Archives show both place of residence and place of enlistment, so that unless the rolls are incorrect, both Keith (and later Plant) enlisted men in the communities where the men lived, often at points distant from Joliet (and Peoria). Certainly they had sub-recruiters in a number of communities; it is also possible that they secured signatures in distant towns but entered them a few days later on the rolls. The pattern for recruiting by Keith and by Plant can be seen in Table 1.

The good captain from Joliet had started out to raise a battery of 152 officers and men, as presumably had Plant, but neither was successful, and their men were ordered consolidated into one unit, and rather than be "Keith's Battery" or "Plant's Battery" or the "Joliet Light Artillery," it was designated Battery I, 2nd Regiment, Illinois Light Artillery.

Keith enlisted 64 men and Plant 37; Keith generally worked the area near Joliet and in Michigan, while Plant worked central Illinois and sometimes in southern Illinois. Of the 102 officers and men who were mustered into service on December 31, 1861, at Camp Butler near Springfield as Battery I, all the officers and noncommissioned officers— with the exception of Plant, who was a 1st Lieutenant—had been recruited by Keith.

What do we know of these men of Battery I? A compilation of information from the original muster rolls reveals some interesting data. Of the 102, all but one stated his age at time of enlisting. The average age was twenty-seven and one-half years, somewhat older than might be expected. The range is shown in Table 2. All but eight of them listed their height. The average height of the original recruits was 5 feet, 7½ inches. The range is shown in Table 3. All but ten of the recruits listed their place of birth. It is interesting to note that more than one-fourth of them had been born abroad (see Table 4). His place of residence was

1. PATTERN OF RECRUITING BY KEITH AND PLANT

Date	No.	Place Enlisted	Residence	Date	No.	Place Enlisted	Residence
		BY KEITH				BY PLANT	
Oct. 20	1	Joliet	Joliet	Nov. 9	1	Camp Butler	Peoria
21	1	Joliet	Joliet	20	1	Clinton	Clinton
25	1	Aurora	Aurora	25	1	Carbondale	Carbondale
25	3	Naperville	Aurora	25	3	Clinton	Clinton
26	1	Pontiac	Pontiac	25	3	Peoria	Peoria
29	1	Joliet	Joliet	Dec. 6	1	Carbondale	Carbondale
Nov. 1	1	Chicago	Chicago	6	5	Clinton	Clinton
1	1	Chicago	Peru	6	4	Decatur	Decatur
1	1	Naperville	Naperville	15	1	Clinton	Clinton
1	3	Lyons, Michigan	Lyons	15	5	Decatur	Decatur
6	1	Chicago	Chicago	15	2	Livingston County	Livingston County
16	3	Joliet	Joliet	15	2	Mt. Vernon	Mt. Vernon
16	1	Lockport	Lockport	15	3	Wapella	Wapella
16	3	Plainfield	Plainfield	26	1	Camp Butler	Sangamon County
16	1	Ionia, Michigan	Ionia	28	1	Camp Butler	Manchester
16	1	Lyons, Michigan	Lyons	29	1	Camp Butler	Decatur
Dec. 1	2	Joliet	Joliet	30	2	Camp Butler	Will County
8	1	Joliet	Joliet				
12	3	Camp Butler	Naperville				
17	1	Joliet	Joliet				
18	1	Aurora	Aurora				
18	1	Joliet	Joliet				
20	1	Joliet	Homer				
28	1	Joliet	Joliet				

2. AGE OF 1861 RECRUITS

Age	No.	Age	No.	Age	No.	Age	No.
18	11	24	9	31	2	40	1
19	5	25	5	32	1	41	1
20	4	26	8	33	5	42	2
21	5	28	9	34	1	43	4
22	6	29	2	35	1	44	2
23	8	30	4	38	1	48	1
						51	2

3. HEIGHT OF 1861 RECRUITS

Height	No.	Height	No.	Height	No.
5 ft. 1 in.	1	5 ft. 6 in.	18	5 ft. 11 in.	8
5 ft. 2 in.	2	5 ft. 7 in.	13	6 ft. 0 in.	2
5 ft. 3 in.	1	5 ft. 8 in.	14	6 ft. 1 in.	1
5 ft. 4 in.	3	5 ft. 9 in.	14	6 ft. 4 in.	1

4. PLACE OF BIRTH OF 1861 RECRUITS

Place	No.	Place	No.
New York	31	Ireland	7
Illinois	13	Germany	4
Ohio	10	Canada	3
Indiana	6	England	3
Massachusetts	2	Scotland	3
Michigan	2	Austria	1
New Jersey	2	France	1
Connecticut	1	Switzerland	1
Pennsylvania	1	Wales	1
Total	68		24

5. PLACE OF RESIDENCE OF 1861 RECRUITS

Residence	No.	Residence	No.	Residence	No.
Joliet	35	Aurora	2	Lockport	1
Clinton	10	Carbondale	2	Peru	1
Decatur	9	Chicago	2	Pontiac	1
Naperville	7	Livingston Cty.	2	Sangamon Cty.	1
Plainfield	5	Mt. Vernon	2	Tuscola	1
Peoria	4	Will Cty.	2	Manchester	1
Wapella	3	Bloomington	1	Ionia, Mich.	1
Channahon	3	Homer	1	Lyons, Mich.	4

6. OCCUPATION OF 1861 RECRUITS

Occupation	No.	Occupation	No.	Occupation	No.
Farmer	43	Merchant	2	Cooper	1
Laborer	13	Miller	2	Joiner	1
Boatman	6	Miner	2	Printer	1
Blacksmith	4	Musician	2	Raftsman	1
Engineer	3	Banker	1	Saddler	1
Carpenter	3	Bricklayer	1	Shoemaker	1
Physician	3	Clerk	1	Tailor	1

7. BATTERY I ORGANIZATION—DESIRED, ACTUAL, AND SPECIFIED

Keith's Goal Sept. 24, 1861	Muster In, Dec. 31, 1861	Specified by War Department Sept. 6, 1862
1 Captain	Captain Charles W. Keith	1 Captain
1 Lieutenant	Senior 1st Lt. Charles M. Barnett	1 1st Lieutenant
1 Lieutenant	Junior 1st Lt. Henry B. Plant	1 2nd Lieutenant
1 Lieutenant	Senior 2nd Lt. Alonzo W. Coe	1 1st Sergeant
1 Lieutenant	Jr. 2nd Lt. William E. Hayward	1 Qm Sergeant
1 Sergeant	1st Sgt. John A. Kelly	4 Sgts
1 Sergeant	Qm. Sgt. Charles D. Haight	8 Corporals
1 Sergeant	Sgt. Rufus S. Stolp	2 Musicians
1 Sergeant	Sgt. Judson Rich	2 Artificers
1 Sergeant	Sgt. Abraham Whitman	1 Wagoner
1 Sergeant	Corp. Hiram W. Hill	122 Privates
1 Sergeant	Corp. Charles Howard	144 *
1 Sergeant	Corp. George F. Ward	
12 Corporals	Corp. Peter Countryman	
2 Buglers	Corp. Robert Heath	
125 Privates	Corp. Marcus D. L. Covert	
152	Artificer Christian G. Geyer	
	Artificer William Bradley	
	84 Privates	
	102	

* One 1st and one 2nd lieutenant, 2 Sgts. and 4 corporals may be added at the president's discretion.

listed by every man but one (see Table 5). All but four reported their marital status: thirty-eight were married; sixty were single. Almost half were farmers; nine did not report an occupation. The range of occupation of the original recruits is shown in Table 6.

The original organization Keith was recruiting to fill was not what he achieved and even with Plant's men, the Battery at muster in totaled only 102 officers and men. Table 7 shows the organization Keith wanted, the organization as best it can be determined from the rolls at muster in, and the organization of a battery as specified by the War Department in General Orders No. 126, Washington, September 6, 1862. By either table of organization, Battery I was always under strength, sometimes seriously so. Being so much under strength bothered the Battery's commanding officer, the officers of the 2nd Regiment of Illinois Light Artillery and some of the commanders of units with which the Battery served, but does not seem to have been a matter of great concern to the Governor of Illinois, the Illinois Adjutant General or other state authorities. In November, 1862, both Captain Charles M. Barnett, commanding Battery I, and William L. Duff, Lt. Colonel, 2nd Illinois Light Artillery, wrote to the Illinois Adjutant General about the shortage of men in Battery I; General Philip Sheridan endorsed Barnett's letter, commending him and the Battery.

LaGrange, Tennessee
November 21, 1862

Col. A. C. Fuller
Adjt. Genl
State of Illinois
Colonel—

 I have this day received the monthly report for October of Battery I, 2nd Ills Arty, Capt. Barnett. It appears that the battery has but 61 men for duty—and but 68 in all including sick in camp and 10 absent sick making an aggregate of Present and Absent 78 men. From this you will see that 72 recruits are wanted to fill up this battery which I hope you will soon be able to supply.

 Lt. Hayward of this battery is on recruiting service in Illinois and has been for months—I do not hear of his doing anything.

 I am anxiously waiting for a reply to my last—Michigan is filling her batteries of which I have three—Ohio also is sending us men—why not Illinois.

Your friend
W. L. Duff
Lt. Col. 2nd Ill Arty

FOREWORD

Nashville, Tenn. Nov. 9th 1862

Sir:

Your letter of October 7th did not reach me until nearly the end of the month – and thinking that my absent Lieutenants, W. E. Hayward and Chas. D. Haight have had time to rejoin, I again beg leave to call your attention to the condition of my Battery

While in Louisville, Ky. two (2) Guns were sent to me and a sufficient number of men detailed from Infantry regiments to enable me to work them. The officers of these Regiments are very anxious to have their men return – and express considerable dissatisfaction at being obliged to send men to the Battery – At the same time I do not want these men, – the artillery service requiring the best of men, which I do not get upon a detail.

From the Generals in the field, under whose command I have been, I have always received whatever I needed, and they could procure; and although we are all from Illinois, and have upheld her honor wherever we were serving, the Battery has not, as yet, received anything from the State.

I sent Lieut. Hayward to Springfield July 7th, to recruit for me. Since his absence he has wrote to the Battery, stating that he had sent recruits, by hundreds, to other Regiments. Lieut. Haight has never joined his Co. since his promotion. – Another of my Lieut. was left in the Hospital at Louisville Oct. 1, and with one Lieut. I fought my Battery from daylight until dark, at Perryville, Oct. 8.

I feel that this incessant care is more than my health will bear – the Battery having, as yet, never moved or fired a gun without my being present

I am compelled, in justice to the brave non-commissioned officers, and men with me to again ask that Lieuts. Hayward and Haight be immediately ordered to return to their command, and there prove themselves capable of filling the position they hold, to the detriment of those good men that have undergone every hardship the service called for.

And I most respectfully ask that Seventy two (72) good men be sent immediately, as I shall be compelled, if I do not receive them soon, to turn over some of my guns. If it is impossible to furnish recruits please write me so, and I shall then cease to expect anything from my State.

I Remain Very Respectfully
Your Obedient Servant
Chas. M. Barnett
Capt. Batt "I" 2nd Ill

To
Adjt Gen. Fuller
Springfield Ill

[Endorsement on back reads:]
Head Quats 11th Division
Army of the Cumberland
I respectfully refer and commend this report to his Excellency
the Governor of Illinois. Capt Barnet & his Battery, is and has been,
an honor to his state—
Your excellency can make no mistake in giving him a cordial
support He is a modest excellent & faithful officer

P H Sheridan
Brig Genrl
Comdg 11th Divs

Recruiting had gone on, however, beginning the day after the Battery was mustered in, with Captain Keith signing up seven men on January 1, 1862; Lt. Plant secured two recruits that same day and Lt. Hayward one. On January 9, Keith signed another, on January 22 Lt. Barnett another; on August 18, Lt. Hayward added another name to the roll, and Lt. Barnett, on September 15, added the last recruit for the year. Altogether, Battery I added only fifteen new men in the entire year of 1862, and eleven of these were enlisted on January 1, just one day too late to join the company at muster in.

The record for 1863 was the same; sixteen new men were added for the year; the last few days of January and the first week of February, 1863, Lt. Coe was in Joliet and Chicago, signing eight men to the roll. On January 29, Abel Longworth, Captain and Provost Marshal of the 6th Illinois District, sent his first man to the Battery from his office in Joliet. Captain Longworth would send seventy men to Battery I before the war ended. May 12 was the day Captain Barnett in Nashville added a recruit, as did Lt. Plant on August 15. Captain James Woodruff, Provost Marshal of the 4th Illinois District, sent a man from Quincy on November 28 and Captain Longworth signed four men from Joliet in the last two weeks of December. And that was all that Battery I received in the way of re-enforcement in 1863.

But to complicate further the manpower situation, the men were asked, at the end of 1863, to re-enlist for three years or the duration of the war, presumably whichever was shorter. After all the pressure that army authorities could bring to bear was exerted, the men talked it over and sixty-four (or sixty-five) of them decided to re-enlist. They made their decision on January 1 and were mustered in on January 3 and immediately sent back to Illinois for thirty-day furloughs. While the men were off on furlough, the officers were sent out to recruit; with help from the district provost marshals, sixty-five new men were signed for service with the Battery before it left for Tennessee on March 4. Captain Longworth sent forty-three men; Lt. Rich two men; Lt. Coe thirteen men; Lt. Plant two men; Major Charles J. Stolbrand of the staff of the 2nd Illinois Light Artillery sent one man; Provost Marshals Davidson, James and Cook each sent one man and Captain Barnett sent one man. In March, three more men were sent to the Battery; in June two old men re-enlisted; in July and August, two men arrived, in September two recruits and in October, eight more; the last man to be added to the unit signed in November. Captain Longworth sent all of the men in 1864 except two forwarded by Captain Isaac Keys, Provost Marshal in the Springfield District, and one signed in Chattanooga by Captain Barnett. To finish the picture of Battery strength, three men signed in Joliet by Captain Longworth were forwarded in January, 1865.

The records of the men added to the battery in 1862 and 1863 are not complete, but the records for the eighty-one men added in 1864 are much better. It is perhaps not surprising to learn that they averaged about two inches less in height (5 feet, 6 inches) and about two years less in age (25 years, 5 months) than the original men of 1861. A higher percentage were born abroad than in the 1861 group (79 of 81 reporting), as shown in Table 8. By occupation, farmers and laborers again accounted for more than half of the 1864 group (78 of 81 reporting), as shown in Table 9.

Table 10, made from the surviving monthly Reports of Battery I, covering a seventeen-month period (July and December, 1864 missing), shows the strength of Battery I. It is impossible to reconcile perfectly these figures with the known recruiting figures for several reasons, one being that men recruited in Illinois were very slow in reaching the battery in the field, and another that men on detached service or sick away from the battery do not always appear promptly in the "Monthly Reports." It is known that men were detailed from other units, particularly from the 2nd Independent Battery, Minnesota Light Artillery, but it is not always known how many and how they were counted. To illustrate this problem of numbers of men, a table in *O. R.*, Series 1, Volume 38, Part 5, page 477, indicates that on March 1, 1864, Battery I had 65

8. PLACE OF BIRTH OF 1864 RECRUITS

Place	No.	Place	No.
New York	13	England	12
Illinois	11	Ireland	8
Ohio	7	Canada	6
Pennsylvania	7	Germany	3
Indiana	4	Bohemia	1
Wisconsin	2	France	1
Connecticut	1	Scotland	1
Kentucky	1	Switzerland	1
Total	46		33

9. OCCUPATION OF 1864 RECRUITS

Occupation	No.	Occupation	No.	Occupation	No.
Farmer	29	Clerk	2	Druggist	1
Laborer	16	Soldier	2	Harnessmaker	1
Carpenter	4	Baker	1	Mason	1
Painter	4	Bartender	1	Mechanic	1
Blacksmith	3	Boatman	1	Molder	1
Sailor	3	Butcher	1	Printer	1
Shoemaker	3	Cooper	1	Teacher	1

veterans and 70 recruits, for a total of 135 men. Another table in *O. R.*, Series 1, Volume 38, Part 5, page 520, shows that on August 15, Battery I had 3 officers and 138 men. A third report, *O. R.*, Series 1, Volume 38, Part 5, page 761, says that on September 1, 1864, Battery I had 3 officers and 137 men, including a "detail of 33 men." Yet another, *O. R.*, Series 1, Volume 38, Part 1, page 824, says on May 5, 1864, Battery I had "for duty" 3 officers and 152 men and on September 5, 1864, 3 officers and 137 men. A fifth report, *O. R.*, Series 1, Volume 44, page 696, assigns on December 12, 1864, 1 officer and 113 enlisted men to Battery I.

How many men served with Battery I from December 31, 1861, to June 14, 1865? It is difficult to say with absolute certainty, but it appears that 102 were mustered in on December 31, 1861, 15 more in 1862, 16 more in 1863; 64 of the original 102 decided to re-enlist in January, 1864, and 2 others re-enlisted later that year, while 81 new men joined the unit in 1864 and 3 more in 1865. The number who served, then, appears to have been 217.

10. BATTERY I MUSTER STRENGTH, JANUARY 1864–MAY 1865

	OFFICERS			ENLISTED			OFFICERS & ENLISTED				ENLISTED ABSENCES				
	on duty	ab-sent	total	on duty	ab-sent	total	on duty	ab-sent	total	total last re-turn	sick	det. serv.	prison or ar-rest	on leave	cap-tured
January 1864		4	4		82	86	0	86	86	87	5	11	2	64	
February 29	2	2	4	72	24	96	74	28	100	86	7	15	2		
March 31	3	2	5	113	12	125	116	14	130	100	9			2	1
April 30	4	1	5	115	7	122	119	8	127	130	5			2	
May 31	3	1	4	118	10	128	121	11	132	127	6	2	2		
June 31	2	2	4	118	15	133	120	17	137	132	10	2	2		1
July									134	137					
August 31	3	1	4	109	20	129	112	21	133	134	19				1
September 30	3	1	4	112	17	129	115	18	133	133	16				1
October	2	2	4	83	36	129	85	38	133	133	13	22			1
November 31	2	1	3	113	16	129	115	17	132	133	14	1			1
December									129	132					
January 31, 1865	1	1	2	109	19	128	110	20	130	129	17	1			1
February 28	1	1	2	112	16	128	113	17	130	130	14	1			1
March 31	1	1	2	110	15	125	111	16	127	130	12	2			1
April	2	1	3	109	15	124	111	16	127	127	12	2			1
May 31	3	0	3	114	10	124	117	10	127	127	10				

Battery I was a light artillery unit, not a "horse" artillery unit; its members, except for the postillions, rode on the ammunition chests, or more often walked. The 2nd Regiment, Illinois Light Artillery, never served as a regiment; each battery served as an independent unit. Battery I was attached to three different armies: the Army of Mississippi, the Army of the Ohio, and the Army of the Cumberland. Its longest service was with the artillery of the 2nd Division, 14th Army Corps, Army of the Cumberland. Usually the Battery was assigned to the artillery of a division, and frequently within the division was assigned to serve with a specific brigade. The trend in Union armies as the war went on was to assign batteries to higher units—corps or armies—and then send them temporarily to lower units as needed. For example, at the beginning of the Atlanta Campaign, the 14th Army Corps had six artillery batteries under Major Charles Houghtaling, Chief of Corps Artillery. Battery I and the 5th Wisconsin Battery were assigned to the 2nd Division, Captain Barnett acting as Chief of 2nd Division artillery. On July 24th all batteries of the 14th Corps were withdrawn from the Divisions and made a separate command under Major Houghtaling—in real-

NET GAIN					NET LOSS								
Off.	Enlisted				Officers					Enlisted			
pro-moted	recruits from depot	enl. in rgt.	from de-sertion	total	resig.	dismis.	dis-ability	G C M	by tr.	KIA or of wounds	dead disease	de-serted	arrested
											1		
	16			16				1			1		
1	28	3	1	32				1		1			
											1	2	
	7		1	8							1	1	
	5			5									
											1		
	2			2			1				1		
		1	1	2	1						1	1	
	3			3						1			1
										1		2	
2	2					1(?)		1	1		1		

ity, directly under the control of the corps commander. The different assignments of the battery are detailed in footnotes.

The Battery had to operate with a variety of weapons as the war progressed. Their first weapons were four James guns which they received soon after arriving at Cairo. The James was a bronze, muzzle-loading, rifled weapon, with a bore of 3.8 inches, that fired a six-pound projectile. While the Battery was at Louisville, Kentucky, two Parrott guns were added, making the Battery a six-gun unit. The new guns, invented by Robert P. Parrott, were muzzle-loading, rifled weapons, with a bore of about 3 inches. They fired a ten-pound projectile. Then at about this same time, or at least prior to the Battle of Perryville, two of the original James guns were replaced by two Napoleons. The Napoleons were bronze, muzzle-loading weapons which fired a twelve-pound projectile.

The Battery used these six guns (2 Jameses, 2 Parrotts, 2 Napoleons) until October 19, 1863, at Chattanooga, where they were replaced by Rodman guns. Made by a method developed by Thomas J. Rodman, these guns were cast iron, muzzle-loading, smooth-bore weapons; with a bore of 3 inches they fired a six-pound projectile. On July 16, 1864, these guns were turned over, and the Battery received regulation three-inch guns. These were muzzle-loading, rifled weapons with a bore of 3 inches, that fired a ten-pound projectile; they were the standard ordnance weapons of the army.

The Battery usually served as a six-gun battery, although from time to time one section of two guns would be on duty away from the others. But beginning with the movement of part of the Battery to Tennessee in September, 1864, the number of guns was reduced to four. This reduction coincided with General Sherman's plan to use four-gun batteries on the March to the Sea; the battery remained a four-gun unit in the final campaign through the Carolinas.

The three men who were responsible for writing this history of Battery I were Thaddeus C. S. Brown, Samuel J. Murphy, and William G. Putney. Not much is known about these three men, particularly after they were mustered out of the army. Thaddeus C. S. Brown was born March 7, 1838, in Watervliet, New York, and was 5 feet 8 inches tall, single, with dark hair, gray eyes, and a fair complexion, and had been a printer when he was enlisted as a private for artillery service by Captain Keith on October 21, 1861, in Joliet. (Some records say Ionia, Michigan, on November 16, 1861.) He was mustered into service at Camp Butler on December 31, 1861.

Brown was a quartermaster sergeant when he re-enlisted as a veteran in Chattanooga, Tennessee, on January 1, 1864. On May 1, 1864, he was on detached service at Headquarters, Chief of Artillery, 2nd Division, 14th Army Corps, and did not return to Battery I until the end of June. On November 15, 1864, he was in Nashville, Tennessee, by order of Major General Thomas, to be examined for a commission. From that date he never rejoined the Battery, being sick and in the hospital either at Louisville or Chicago. On June 8, 1865, Brown wrote from a hospital in Chicago to the Governor of Illinois, saying in part:

> The Surgeon in charge of this hospital thinks he will have to dis-
> charge me on certificate of disability—(he has, however, written
> to Department Head Qrs. for further information in regard to
> it,);—but I will not accept a discharge on account of disability
> (Deafness) if I am entitled to my "muster out," for this reason, viz:
>
> If I accept a discharge on account of *disability*, I lose the balance
> of *veteran bounty* remaining unpaid—but which I would receive, if
> I am *mustered out*,—as do all the members of my battery.

Such being the facts in the case I have the honor to hope that you can have me *mustered out*, at this place, under orders from the War Dept.

This plea did Sgt. Brown no good, for he was discharged on certificate of disability, June 26, 1865.

He was married, June 28, 1871, in Toledo, Ohio, to Jane E. Hubbard; the couple had two children, a daughter, Ina F. A. Brown, born May 9, 1872, died in December, 1910, in Chicago and a son, Samuel H. Brown, born June 11, 1874, in Chicago. After his discharge, Brown lived in Chicago, working as a printer; in 1919 he required constant care, suffering from a double hernia, and being almost totally deaf and blind. He died in Chicago on January 22, 1927, and was buried in Joliet.

Samuel J. Murphy was born June 20, 1834, in Reading, Pennsylvania, and was 5 feet 9 inches tall, married, with black hair, gray eyes, and a fair complexion, and had been a farmer when he was enlisted as a sergeant by Captain Barnett on January 1, 1862, in Jacksonville, Illinois. His post office address had been Petersburg, Illinois. Murphy re-enlisted as a veteran in Chattanooga, Tennessee, on January 1, 1864. On January 23, while Murphy was home on furlough, five prominent Petersburg men petitioned the Governor to give him a higher position. The Governor noted on the letter: "Gen. Fuller—File this carefully to be considered whenever chance for promotion for this Sergeant." Murphy was divorced from his wife, Sarah Matilda Fox, in Petersburg in 1864, probably at this time. Murphy was sent to Nashville in March, 1865, by order of Major General Thomas, to appear before an "examining board for officers for colored artillery Batteries." Apparently he was to be sent as a first lieutenant to a Negro artillery battery, but the approaching end of the war prevented this promotion. He returned to the Battery sometime in May and was mustered out as a sergeant at Camp Butler on June 14, 1865. Murphy married again, this time to Alice Adelia Rexford on December 28, 1868, near Momence, Illinois. The couple had two children, a boy, Cullen B. Murphy, born December 23, 1875; and Helen E. Murphy, born September 14, 1884. He lived in Petersburg and in Kankakee County, Illinois; in Rush City, Minnesota; in Kansas; in Siloam Springs, Arkansas; and finally in Donalda, Alberta, Canada, where he died, January 8, 1918.

William G. Putney was born at South Bridge, Massachusetts, July 2, 1842, and was 5 feet 9 inches tall, single, with blue eyes, light hair, and a fair complexion, and had been a farmer when he was enlisted as a private by Captain Keith on October 1, 1861, in Channahon, Illinois. His post office address then was Minooka, Illinois. He was mustered into service December 31, 1861, at Camp Butler. Putney, who served as a bugler, re-enlisted as a veteran on January 1, 1864, in Chattanooga, Tennessee. He served with the battery until January 20, 1865, when he entered a hospital in Savannah, Georgia, suffering from an eye disease and hernia. He was discharged in Savannah on May 20, 1865, on a surgeon's certificate of disability.

Putney was a physician, and lived in Kendall, Grundy, and La Salle counties in Illinois, and moved to Lincoln, Nebraska, on June 10, 1904. He was married to Cornelia Elizabeth Boomer in Bristol (now Yorkville), Illinois on March 13, 1873. The couple had five children, Lucy, born in 1875; Nelie A., born March 13, 1876; James W., born February 14, 1878; John F., born April 21, 1880; Charles R., born January 24, 1887. The couple also raised a foster son named Harry Farbush. Dr. Putney died while visiting his son John in Winner, South Dakota, October 27, 1919.

In the Preface Dr. Putney points out that Brown and Murphy had "first outlined and partially written" the history of Battery I and that Brown then worked with the material until the history "began to take shape as a fair representation of what Battery I did to help preserve the Union." Dr. Putney then "added many items and anecdotes" and, as he puts it, "typewrote it into book form." His most substantial contributions were not the anecdotes but his descriptions of the battles of Perryville and Chickamanga. This history is, in a very real sense, the product of all three men; Dr. Putney did what amounts to a kind of personal editorial job.

The manuscript is presented here with only a minimum of editorial interference. Sentence structure remains as in the original, but since Brown, Murphy, and Putney together or singly seem limited in their knowledge of orthography, spelling corrections have been made, the first time in square brackets next to the misspelled word, as Murphey [Murphy]. If the word is misspelled more than once, it is corrected the second and later times without benefit of brackets. The first name and middle initial of an individual is inserted in square brackets the first time the individual appears, as: S. J. Murphy [Samuel J. Murphy]; if the name appears again, it appears as in the manuscript unless misspelled. In the few instances in which the dates are incorrect, they are

corrected either in footnotes or by the correct date in square brackets
following the incorrect date, as: May 15 [May 16]. Finally, to avoid an
excess of footnotes, short chapter introductions have been added; short
biographical notes about each Battery I man mentioned are inserted as
an appendix.

The reader will smile at the wordings "brave bugler" and "brave
bugler Putney" but will be less amused to learn that several times the
authors borrowed from published works and forgot to mention that
they borrowed. They—or at least Dr. Putney—were familiar with the
articles in the old *Century Magazine* "Century War Series," Sherman's
Memoirs, and Woodruff's *Fifteen Years Ago: or, the Patriotism of
Will County.* The acknowledged quotes in the original manuscript are
often inaccurate; they have been corrected for publication. All three of
the authors were absent from the battery for the Carolina campaign,
and the original last chapter, covering this campaign, was nothing more
than a compilation of quotes, some acknowledged, and others not. It
has seemed best to substitute the battery diary, kept on the monthly
reports, and Lt. Judson Rich's *Report* for this chapter, except for
Dr. Putney's last few pages, which are used to end the narrative.

I am indebted to a number of people for their help in preparing this
manuscript for publication. First and foremost is Mr. James S. Schoff,
who not only owns the original manuscript, but whose financial assistance has made its publication possible. Mrs. Byron Levene and Mr.
David Follmer of the Civil War Centennial Commission of Illinois were
always ready to answer troublesome questions, as were Miss Margaret
A. Flint and Mrs. Mildred Schulz of the Illinois State Historical
Library. Miss Mary Lynn McCree of the Illinois State Archives
never failed to locate elusive records; Mrs. Louis Darovec and Mrs.
Bernard Brennan faithfully typed and retyped the manuscript. And
once again, I am indebted to Mrs. Barbara Long for her excellent maps.

Springfield, Illinois
July 16, 1964

PREFACE

by W. G. Putney

THE HISTORY OF BATTERY I is only one of many that may and have been written of hundreds of regiments and batteries that took an active part in the Great War of the Rebellion.

Each man who served during that eventful period feels that he would like to have his relatives, children and friends know how well the organization in which he was one of many that bravely acted their part, had helped to restore order to what was once a slave-ridden, war-distracted country over which "Old Glory" should forever float with pride and honor.

The History was first outlined and partially written by Quartermaster T. [Thaddeus] C. S. Brown and Sergeant S. J. Murphey [Samuel J. Murphy]. They did the best they could to find data and material from different diaries and reports; also searched the War Records; but few of the officers or men kept complete daily records of the movements of the battery, and those that had them were either dead, or their friends or families had failed to save as they should such valuable papers. Other members of the battery that had kept diaries could not be located or found.

Quartermaster Brown labored indefatigably in compiling, writing and re-writing, until the material began to take shape as a fair representation of what Battery I did to help preserve the Union. The manuscript was finally turned over to Bugler W. [William] G. Putney, who again added many items and anecdotes to its pages, and at the same time typewrote it into book form.

All feel that the work is far from being a perfect and complete history, but as a memorial of a time that tried the Saxon grit of the

PREFACE

sons of a Young Republic and the resources of a liberty-loving people, it shall send its little light into the great world of historical literature, probably not to interest the masses, but those that had friends, brothers and fathers, that served nobly and well in the ranks of Battery I.

W. G. Putney.

Serena, Illinois
January 1st, 1897

BEHIND THE GUNS

The History of Battery I, 2ⁿᵈ Regiment

Illinois Light Artillery

1

BATTERY I
IS MUSTERED INTO SERVICE

In which Battery I, 2nd Illinois Light Artillery is organized from units raised by Charles W. Keith, of Joliet and Henry B. Plant, of Peoria. Battery I is mustered into service at Camp Butler, near Springfield, Illinois, on December 31, 1861, and leaves Camp Butler for Cairo, Illinois, at the juncture of the Ohio and Mississippi Rivers, on February 7, 1862. Here the Battery trains until March 7, when it heads down river for attack on New Madrid, Missouri, and Island Number 10. Captain Keith resigns on April 7 and Lieutenant Charles M. Barnett assumes command of the Battery. After New Madrid and Island Number 10 capitulate, the Battery goes down the river to Ft. Pillow, but is recalled to participate in Major General Henry W. Halleck's advance toward Corinth, Mississippi.

IN THE FALL of 1861 Charles W. Keith, of Joliet, Ills., received a Captain's commission from Governor [Richard] Yates, and was authorized to recruit a battery of light artillery. He opened a recruiting office at Joliet, and appointed men as recruiting officers at other points near Joliet to enlist men for the battery for three years' service. The first enlistments were made October 1st, 1861. The recruits, as fast as enlisted, were forwarded to Camp Butler,[1] located about four miles east of Springfield, Ills.

1.   Camp Butler, some four miles east of Springfield, was named for William Butler, then State Treasurer of Illinois. Originally located six miles east of Springfield on Clear Lake, the first troops occupied Camp Butler on August 5, 1861. Prior to August 5, troops were quartered on the fairgrounds at what was called Camp Yates. In the fall of 1861, Camp Butler was moved to the great Western R.R. tracks near Riverton, Illinois. The camp was used not only as the principle center for assembling and training Illinois troops but as a prison camp. The first Confederate prisoners reached Camp Butler on February 23, 1862.—See Helen Edith Shipley, "Camp Butler in the Civil War Days," *Journal of the Illinois State Historical Society*, XXV, No. 4 (January, 1933), 285-317.

About the same time Henry B. Plant, of Peoria, Ills., was empowered by Governor Yates to raise a battery for the war. December 31st, 1861, the men enlisted by Charles W. Keith, and Henry B. Plant were consolidated into one company, named Keith's Battery, and mustered into the United States service as Battery I 2nd Ill. Regt. Light Artillery. The roster of officers was as follows: Charles W. Keith, Captain; Charles M. Barnett, Sr. 1st Lieutenant; Henry B. Plant, Jr. 1st Lieutenant; Alonzo W. Coe, Sr. 2nd Lieutenant; William E. Hayward, Jr. 2nd Lieutenant.

During November and December the men were drilled in detachments, stood guard and performed other duties pertaining to camp life; the men were also detailed to build barracks for winter quarters.

December 15th, '61, thirty men, under Lieutenant Barnett, were detailed for duty at the State armory at Springfield, Ill., and remained there until the 19th, when they were relieved by another detachment from Camp Butler. While at the armory the men had their first drill at the gun.

December 23rd an order was issued by [Illinois] Adjutant General [Allan C.] Fuller, that all companies of infantry and battery organizations be immediately filled up and mustered into the United States service, so they could receive pay.

December 27th, the barracks being partly finished, the men in Camp Butler were ordered to move in, and finish them afterwards. The change from the cold tents to the comfortable barracks was a pleasant one, as the weather had been very disagreeable for three or four weeks.[2] Rain and snowstorms, cooking their meals out of doors and sleeping in cold cheerless tents, disgusted many of the men, and

2.   James F. Drish, Lt. Colonel of the 32nd Illinois Infantry, wrote to his wife about conditions at Camp Butler on December 4, 1861 (Drish papers, Illinois State Historical Library, Springfield):

> Our Boys are a greateel more comfortable than You would think the weather being So cold it is realy amusing to walk through our camp and See the Stick chimneys Sticking out of Each tent. for the Boys have Built themselves a kind of furnace of mud Sod and Sticks that make there tents perfectly warm and they have constructed them so nicely that they draw as well as a Stove and perfectly free from Smoke and as the weather has ben so inclement for the last week we have done but little drilling and the Boys have nothing to do But enjoy the fire read & write letters home etc

they longed for the comfortable homes they had given up to fight for the old flag and help put down the rebellion; but safely housed in the rude barracks they were more contented, and only longed for marching orders for the front.

January 3rd, '62, orders were issued from camp headquarters, calling in all men on furloughs, and to be prepared for marching orders; but no marching orders were then received, and there was no telling when the battery would be ordered to the front. Having received four James' rifled brass guns the men were drilled in battery foot tactics, whenever the weather would permit, and they became very proficient in handling the guns.

January 14th United States regulation artillery uniforms were received and donned by the men, as heretofore they had been supplied with infantry uniforms. January 18th the men received their first payment from "Uncle Sam," and were paid in gold and silver, for the first and last time during their long service.

Batteries G, H, and K of the 2nd Ills. Regiment, commanded respectively by Captains Charles J. Stolbrand, Andrew Stenbeck, and Benjamin F. Rogers, were in camp at the same time with Battery I, and each battery took its turn firing the morning and evening gun for the camp.

On February 6th marching orders were received by the different batteries, the guns were loaded on flat cars and sent to Cairo in advance of the men, and on the morning of the 7th the battalion was ordered aboard a passenger train, which, about noon, pulled out while the boys with many hearty cheers bid good bye to old Camp Butler, and were off to the front by the way of Cairo.[3]

The Snow storm that you had in Carlinville did not reach Camp Butler we had a little Snow fall yesterday morning but only aneough to make the Ground look a little white.

I took a trip out to the new Barracks this afternoon they look like comfort compared with tents they are being built Some three miles from here on the Great Western RailRod & about four miles from Springfield they are Said to Be the Best Barracks in the country and on the Best ground. I think we will be able to move into them this week.

3.   (Springfield) *Illinois State Journal*, February 8, 1862: "That part of the 2nd regiment of light artillery, which has been stationed at Camp Butler, left for Cario [sic] by the Great Western Railroad yesterday. Col. Mather, Lieut. Col. Duff, Maj. Starring, Maj. Stollbrand, and Adjutant Higgins, accompanied the battalion, which consisted of about 400 men, the cannon caissons, etc., for the battalion also went down by special freight train."

BEHIND THE GUNS

Old Camp Butler, how many of the men that left you that day never saw you again. There they had received their first lessons in the rudiments of war, and felt the first light privations of home comforts, did their first guard duty and grumbling at their officers, also patient, long-suffering "Old Uncle Sam." Few of them, as they were whirled away from its shelter, seemed to realize that soon, very soon, they were to receive their baptism of blood, and learn what grim visaged war was in earnest. All they knew and cared to know was, that they were bound for the front, soon to show their country and the loved ones at home, that they were "True blue," and that "Johnny Reb" would have a chance to see the kind of metal the "Yanks" were made of. Three months of the dull routine of camp life had become irksome to the men, and they were glad of the change.

The train containing the four batteries arrived at Cairo about nine in the forenoon on the 8th, but the men were kept in the cars until two o'clock in the afternoon, when they were ordered to unload their guns from the flat cars. No place for a camp having been found, about five o'clock the officers took possession of some freight cars on the Illinois Central tracks, in which the men, after supper, having procured some hay for bedding, turned in for the night.

On the 9th the battery, with the rest of the battalion, crossed the Ohio River, and went into camp on the Kentucky shore about a mile and a half above Fort Holt. The camp was called Camp Paine.

The roster of commissioned and non-commissioned officers of the battery at this time was as follows: Charles W. Keith, Captain; Charles M. Barnett, Sr. 1st Lieutenant; Henry B. Plant, Jr. 1st Lieutenant; Alonzo W. Coe, Sr. 2nd Lieutenant; William E. Hayward, Jr. 2nd Lieutenant; John A. Kelly, Orderly Sergeant; Charles D. Haight, Quartermaster Sergeant; Rufus S. Stolp, Judson Rich, Charles McDonald, and George T. Ward, Sergeants; Gunners: Abraham Whitmore [Whitman], Hiram W. Hill, S. J. Murphy, Robert Heath. Chief of Caissons: Charles Howard, Peter Countryman, Marcus D. L. Covert, and William Haines. Charles D. Haight Quartermaster Sergeant, was left at Springfield on detached duty at the Adjutant General's headquarters, and Captain Keith appointed T. C. S. Brown, Acting Quartermaster Sergeant, which place he held until Haight was promoted to Lieutenant, when Captain Barnett promoted him to the office.

Signs of war were all around, but the men were not yet satisfied; they were not at the fighting front. (Such is human nature.) The officers were back and forth from Cairo every day, getting the battery in shape for the field, trying to get horses for the guns.

February 13th forty-eight men were detached from the battalion, twelve from each battery, with ten days rations, to go on the mortar boats up the Cumberland River to Fort Donalson [Donelson], on which [Brigadier] General [Ulysses S.] Grant was then moving. Lieutenant Barnett was given the command of the detachment from Battery I.

While the detail was gone the officers in charge of the camp were very strict, and a strong guard was posted around the artillery park, and the guards instructed to allow no one to pass in. One night Major [Charles J.] Stolbrand who had command of the camp, to try the discipline of the men, went outside the camp, and in coming in undertook to pass the guard at post number three, where he was halted by Roger [Rogers] Cunningham who stood at that post; Stolbrand told the guard who he was, but that made no difference to Cunningham, as he made the Major mark time for about five minutes. The Major urged him to call the corporal of the guard, but Rogers told him that he would take care of him, and kept the Major marking time with his old Belgian rifle pointed at him. After Rogers had amused himself at the Major's expense long enough he called for the corporal, but as the corporal, S. J. Murphy, did not seem to recognize the Major, the sergeant of the guard was called, who passed him in. The next day the Major sent for the corporal and the guard, and complimented them on their strictness in obeying orders, saying, "That with such men on guard the camp was safe."

To further test the courage of the men a little scare was gotten up. The men were told that the rebels were on their way to attack the camp. The guard was doubled, a detail made for picket duty, and ordered to fall in, and marched at nine o'clock at night to Fort Holt. The rain was pouring down, and through the mud and water, knee deep, the men stumbled and waded, but nothing could dampen their ardor. Each one, full of patriotic zeal felt that without him the camp would be lost. On arriving at Fort Holt the men met their first enemy, the pugnacious "Grayback." The quarters were full of them, and very hungry ones too. The 4th Reg't. Ills. cavalry had occupied the fort for some time, but had left long before the artillery men arrived, and they found the "graybacks" without "rations," ready on the arrival of the battery boys to help themselves to a rich feast on the well fed and fattened men, much to their dismay and torture. Of course no rebels appeared, so the next day the men were ordered back to camp.

About this time the men who had gone up to Fort Donelson on the mortar boats returned to camp. To the men who had remained those that had gone on the expedition came back as heroes, and, of course, their description of their trip and the surrender of the fort was eagerly listened to by squads that gathered round each veteran of so short a campaign. These men had seen a few dead rebels and heard the distant roar of battle, though they failed to reach the fort till after its surrender.

A few days later the prisoners captured at Fort Donelson began to arrive at Cairo, and as many of the battery boys as could get passes availed themselves of the privilege to cross over the river to Cairo for the purpose of seeing the "Johnnies." The boys came to the conclusion, after seeing them, that the Rebs were not as savage as they had been painted. They looked about the same as our men, only a little the worse for wear, and as if they would like to be out of the hands of the "Yankee Mudsills," the name given to Northern soldiers by the South. While in camp here a few of the men were taken sick with the measles, and were sent to the hospital at Cairo. They never returned to the battery, no doubt, receiving their discharge from the army, while at the hospital. Drills and guard duty were the orders of the day, while the batteries were waiting for their horses.

4.   Prior to this time, Battery I had been assigned to the District of Cairo, commanded by Brigadier General Ulysses S. Grant from August 1, 1861 to February 14, 1862. He was succeeded by Brigadier General William T. Sherman, February 14, 1862–March 8, 1862. Colonel Napoleon Bonaparte Buford commanded the Flotilla Brigade of the Army of the Mississippi; this Army was organized February 23, 1862, and

BATTERY I IS MUSTERED INTO SERVICE

On March 3rd news of the evacuation of Columbus, Ky. was received, and it was reported, that, as soon as horses could be procured, the battery would be ordered down the river. The men anxiously awaited their arrival. March 4th two companies of the 2nd. and 4th. Michigan cavalry, and the 51st Illinois Infantry, which had been in camp with the batteries, were ordered to break camp and march.

Captain Keith arrived in camp from Cairo, March 6th, and told the men that they would leave for Columbus the next day, and that there were one hundred and ten horses ready in Cairo for the battery, it being the first to receive that, then, so considered favor. The horses arrived the afternoon of the 7th, and, in the evening, the steamer *Illinois* took on board the battery, and steamed down the river, leaving Camp Paine as a thing of the past with a hearty "good bye" from the men. The steamer arrived at Columbus about midnight, March 8th, and at nine in the forenoon the battery landed. It was assigned to Colonel R. N. [Napolean Bonaparte] Buford's command, and directed to make their camp in what was a deserted town.[4] Orders were received on the 14th to "strike" tents and be ready to move, but the steamer did not arrive, on which the battery was to take passage, so the tents were "pitched" again, and the battery waited till the morning of the 15th, when, as the steamer had put in its appearance, all was loaded and proceeded down the river to Hickman's Landing, twelve miles below Columbus. A short stop was made there, long enough to see some very much excited rebels who made bold to cheer for Jeff Davis, and the next moment were flying for their lives before a warlike demonstration of the battery and the infantry on board of the boat. Dropping down the river from that point, the steamer tied up on the Kentucky shore just above the fleet of gunboats commanded by Admiral [Flag Officer Andrew H.] Foote, which was operating on the rebel batteries on the Kentucky shore, a little above Island No. 10, in the Mississippi River. The

commanded by Major General John Pope, February 23, 1862–June 26, discontinued on October 26, 1862. The Flotilla Brigade consisted of these troops: 27th and 42nd Illinois Infantry, 15th Wisconsin Infantry, Battery G, 1st Illinois Light Artillery, and Battery I, 2nd Illinois Light Artillery.

battery was now a part of [Major] General [John] Pope's command above the Island, the main part of his army being at New Madrid which is below on the Missouri shore. After the men had gotten their dinner on the bank the boat then moved across the river to the Missouri side, and tied up for the night.

On the morning of the 16th the mortar boats were moved down the river to a point above and opposite the Island, where they began firing. The afternoon of the 17th the steamer dropped down to a position between two mortar boats, where at about three o'clock, the battery was landed and moved across the point to the shore opposite the Island. One gun was ordered forward into battery, and opened fire on the enemy's massive works on Island No. 10, with the purpose of drawing the fire of their heavy artillery.[5] The "Johnnies" were not slow in responding to the challenge with solid shot and grape from sixty four and one hundred pound siege guns. It was the first baptism of fire for the boys and a very warm reception at that, but they stood bravely to their gun and did the best they could with their light field piece. Soon Corporal Charles Howard was struck in the right knee by a three pound grape shot, which shattered the joint and mortally wounded him. Lieutenant Barnett then ordered the gun to "limber up" and fall back out of range, having accomplished all that was required, that being to unmask the rebel guns and develop their number and calibre.

Amidst the increased fire of the mortars along side and the whistling sixty four pound shells sent from the Island batteries, the battery was loaded on to the steamer *Graham*, which then moved farther up the river out of range. Charles Howard died that night at nine o'clock, in an unconscious condition, never recovering from the

5.   "This was the only land battery at the north end of the island, and took its position on the Missouri shore within three-fourth of a mile of the powerful guns of the enemy."—George H. Woodruff, *Fifteen Years Ago: or, the Patriotism of Will County* (Joliet: Joliet Republican Book and Job Steam Printing House, 1876), p. 424. This work will be cited hereafter as *Woodruff*.

6.   The 27th Illinois had come down the river on the *Illinois*, arriving at Columbus, Kentucky, on March 4. The 27th left Columbus on March 14 on the steamer *Silver Wave*, stopped at Hickman and then went down to Island No. 10. At least some of the 27th were on the steamer *Silver Wave* while others were on the steamer *T. L. McGill* in the period March 18–22.—See Robert J. Kerner, "The Diary of Ed-

shock of the wound. He was the first of the battery to offer up his life as a sacrifice for his country's welfare and glory. His death cast a gloom over the men of the battery, for a time, in sorrow for the loss of one of their comrades. The morning of the 18th Lieutenant Barnett, with a detail of twelve men, took the remains of Howard down to the point in a boat, where under the shrieking shells of the mortars, and amid the roar of guns from rebel and union batteries, they dug a grave and laid his body away to await the last Great Grand Review.

From the 18th to the 22nd of March the battery was cooped up on the *Graham* with the 27th Illinois infantry, during which time the gunboats and mortars boats were shelling the rebel works on the Island and on the Kentucky shore.[6]

March 23rd the steamer *Graham* moved up the river about a mile, and the battery horses were taken off the boat and exercised. March 24th the battery went aboard the steamer *R. & J. D.*, which proceeded up the river about a mile, and then tied up for the night. The morning of the 25th the battery went ashore with all its camp equipage and established a camp on the bank of the river.

March 27th Captain Keith went to Cairo and returned on the 31st, and left again April 2nd, with the intention of resigning.

While in camp the men put in their time drilling, and soon became proficient in handling their Six pound James rifled pieces, looking and acting like old soldiers.

April 4th tents were "struck" and "Down the river again." April 7th Captain Keith's resignation was accepted, and Lieutenant Barnett assumed command of the battery.[7] The same day Island No. 10 surrendered with 6,700 prisoners, among them were three

ward W. Crippen, Private 27th Illinois Volunteers, War of the Rebellion, August 7, 1861, to September 19, 1863," *Transactions of the Illinois State Historical Society for the Year 1909* (Springfield, 1910), pp. 220–82.

7. As early as January 24, 1862, Governor Richard Yates was receiving mail that urged if Captain Keith resigned, Lt. Charles M. Barnett should be appointed Captain. David M. Casey, an influential citizen of Joliet, wrote on January 24th; Keith himself recommended Barnett on April 10 in a letter to the Governor. Casey wrote again, pointing out Barnett was "sober, honest and faithful," and had been a guard at the penitentiary "2 or 3 years." On June 6, Lt. Colonel William L. Duff (second in command of the 2nd Regiment, Illinois Light Artillery) wrote

Generals and 272 field and company officers. There were over one hundred heavy siege guns, and twenty four pieces of field artillery; also there were several thousand stands of small arms captured.

The battery went into camp on the Island, and on the 10th Lieutenant Barnett, with a detail from his cannoneers as guards, took a boat load of prisoners to Cairo. April 10th Acting Quartermaster Sergeant Brown and Corporal Countryman, who had been to Cairo to dispose of some supplies, rejoined the battery. April 12th the battery went aboard the steamer *Rover*, a boat captured from the rebels on the surrender of Island No. 10. About 10:00 in the forenoon, the *Antelope* arrived from Cairo with Lieutenant Barnett and the cannoneers. All the battery then went aboard the *Antelope* which proceeded down the river to join the fleet, where it arrived about nine in the forenoon on the 14th, and tied up about seven miles above Fort Pillow, on the Arkansas shore. The battery remained there till the 17th, when the *Antelope*, with battery on board, was ordered up the river, arriving at New Madrid on the 18th, where the boat laid too for the night.

the Governor, asking these promotions to be made: Charles M. Barnett to be Captain; Henry B. Plant to be Senior 1st Lieutenant; Alonzo W. Coe to be Junior 1st Lieutenant; W. E. Hayward to be Senior 2nd Lieutenant; Charles D. Haight to be Junior 2nd Lieutenant.

On the back of Duff's letter Governor Yates had written: "Issue Commissions." Curiously enough, on Captain Keith's letter of April 10, Yates had written: "If no objection issue commission." Then he added "Perhaps better wait a while."

Perhaps unaware of all this, Lt. Barnett wrote Yates asking for promotion to Captain, and on the back of this letter a clerk in the Illinois Adjutant General's office had written: "Promotion made in regular order before receipt of this." Barnett's promotion was made to date from May 1, 1862, but no one remembered to tell him, because on June 25, 1862, Barnett sent another letter to Yates—requesting promotion—through channels; Generals Asboth and Elliott endorsed his request. Governor Yates endorsed the letter "If no objection let commission issue" and at the bottom a clerk has noted: "Issued long since." When the commission reached Barnett is not known.

2

EARLY CAMPAIGNS
AND GARRISON DUTY

In which Battery I returns from the expedition to Ft. Pillow and arrives at Hamburg Landing, Tennessee, to participate in the campaign against Corinth, Mississippi. The Battery is split temporarily, with part serving with a Missouri Battery and part with another Illinois Battery; it is reunited on June 14, 1862. It participates in Colonel Philip H. Sheridan's famous fight at Booneville, Mississippi, and is involved in an episode in which mutiny is threatened.

POPE'S ARMY being ordered to reinforce [Major General Henry W.] Halleck's force in front of Corinth, Mississippi,[1] a fleet of transports conveyed the troops on the river, up the Tennessee River to Hamburg Landing [Tennessee]. The battery, on board the

1.   The Battle of Shiloh, April 6–7, 1862, after an initial defeat of the Union troops, ended with the Confederate forces being driven from the field. Major General Henry W. Halleck made an extremely slow and careful advance toward Corinth, Mississippi, the point to which the Confederates had retired after Shiloh. Halleck had recalled the Ft. Pillow expedition to participate in the advance on Corinth.

Antelope, proceeded up the Mississippi River as far as Hickman, Kentucky, where she tied up for the night. The Mississippi River was very high from spring floods, and was still rising, being two feet higher than the high water mark of the year, 1858. The 19th the boat had left New Madrid, the 20th she cast off from Hickman at four o'clock in the morning, and at Columbus Lieutenant Coe rejoined the battery, having been absent about six weeks. Cairo was reached at two in the afternoon, where a stay was made till the 22nd, when the *Antelope* proceeded up the Ohio and the Tennessee, to Clifton which is about forty miles below Pittsburg Landing, arriving there at nine in the evening on the 23rd. Left Clifton at three in the morning on the 24th, and arrived at Hamburg Landing at eleven the same forenoon.

The battery was unloaded and went into camp, tents were pitched, and the men began to enjoy *terra firma*, which they had not felt for some time having been cramped up on a river steamer for over two weeks. Soon campkettles were boiling with fragrant coffee, and bacon was hissing in the frying pans over blazing coals, while the horses and mules were having their feed, standing on the soft fresh earth, instead of the close-penned deck on which they had so long stood. With shouts of exhilaration and joy the men sat down to eat a meal free from steam and coal smoke with the remark, "This begins to look like soldiering."

The stay at the Landing was short, for on the morning of the 26th the battery was ordered to the front, but after a short day's march camp was made for the night. The daily heavy rains had made the roads almost impassable, so that with Halleck's tactics and the condition of the cartpaths, the advance on Corinth was slow. May 2nd an advance of five miles was made, then camped for the night. The battery was attached to [Brigadier] General [Eleazer A.] Paine's Division,[2] and served with it for a short time, but the most of the service in front of Corinth was with the artillery brigade under the command of Lieutenant Colonel [William] Duff, Chief of

2.   The Flotilla Brigade was a part of General Eleazer A. Paine's 4th Division of the Army of the Mississippi. After the fall of Island No. 10 the battery reverted to the Artillery Division of the Army of the Mississippi, commanded by Lt. Colonel William Duff of Illinois.

Artillery for Pope's command, and Lieutenant Colonel of the 2nd Regiment of Artillery, Illinois Volunteers.

General Pope's corps [Army] was the left wing of the army, and he advanced his force more rapidly than Halleck intended, so on the 6th of May, General Paine's division was attacked in front of Farmington by the rebels, and driven back a short distance with the loss of a few prisoners.

On the 8th another advance was made and the battery was ordered to the front, but took no part in the action, and soon returned to camp. The infantry pickets were driven in on the 9th, but the rebels were soon repulsed and order restored.

May 16th orders were received to divide the battery. One section was attached to Captain [John W.] Powell's Regular battery, and the other section to Captain [Henry] Hescock's Missouri battery.[3] The order almost created a mutiny. The men refused to obey the order, when a battalion of infantry was ordered to surround the battery, upon which the two sections marched to their respective commands, though they could not then, nor ever after, understand why the battery should have been divided.

Captain Barnett and Lieutenant Coe went with the first section to Captain Powell, while Lieutenant Plant and Lieutenant Hayward, with the other section, went to Captain Hescock. Both Captain Powell and Captain Hescock treated the men well, and claimed that they had nothing to do with the orders, and allowed each section to hold their own organization intact, each having their own roll-call, and to make their details for guard and fatigue duties, also for drawing rations. The men of Lieutenant Plant's section were so well pleased with the change, that when Captain Barnett sent his orderly sergeant, John Kelly, with a petition, asking that the two sections be united, for the men to sign, they refused to sign it.

Captain Barnett's section was placed on the extreme left of Pope's corps, in breastworks, while Lieutenant Plant's was more to the right, and therefore was under the rebel fire during the siege, if

3.   Captain John W. Powell commanded Battery F, 2nd Illinois Light Artillery, while Captain Henry Hescock commanded Battery G, 1st Missouri Light Artillery.

so it may be called. On the 28th [29–30] of May the rebel army evacuated Corinth, and the morning of the 29th [30th] Pope's forces started in pursuit. Barnett's section was in the advance, and marched all that day close to the vanguard, going into camp at night on the bank of the Tuscumbia River, at which place the advance ran into a masked battery and a number of soldiers were wounded.[4] The next day and night were spent in following the retreat of the rebels, reaching Booneville about daylight, where burned cars and charred gunbarrels gave evidence of the cavalry raid of a few days before. The section camped in the edge of Booneville, and the 2nd of June went with a reconnoitering force towards Baldwin, but returned to camp the same day. The 4th it went with the cavalry under Sheriden [Colonel Philip H. Sheridan], west of Booneville, to Blackland, where a division of rebels was run into, and after a short skirmish the Union force retired to Booneville.[5] Just as one of the guns was retreating from an open field into the road a rebel shell exploded overhead, and a piece struck Allen B. Hodge, a postillion, on the hip, producing a severe wound, from which he suffers to this day. He was the only one injured in either section during the campaign about Corinth. [General Pierre G. T.] Beauregard's forces continued to retreat as far south as Guntown, but no further effort was made to follow them. The Union forces, most of them, fell back to Corinth, while the cavalry remained at Booneville, and a division of troops under [Brigadier] General [Alexander S.] Asboth stopped at Rienza [Rienzi] as an outpost.

June 14th, a month after the two sections had been separated, Lieutenants Plant and Hayward were ordered to report to Captain Barnett for duty with their section. The two sections united while on the road to Rienzi, Miss., and reached that place about two in the afternoon, where Captain Barnett reported for duty to General Asboth, commandant at that place.

June 27th special order, No. 110, from general headquarters,

4.   Battery I had two men wounded on May 30, 1862.—See *Woodruff*, p. 424.

5.   Sheridan mentions this action on pp. 150–52 of Vol. I of his *Memoirs.*—See Philip H. Sheridan, *Personal Memoirs of P. H. Sheridan*, 2 vols. (New York: Charles L. Webster and Company, 1882). This work will be cited hereafter as *Sheridan*.

16

was received, detailing Lieutenant Hayward on recruiting service, ordering him to report to Governor Yates, of Illinois; but he did not get away until about the 1st of July.

In July Sergeant Rich was promoted to orderly sergeant. During this month a very exciting incident occurred in the battery. Andrew Hogan, a postillion on one of the guns, becoming intoxicated, and feeling that his team had not received their requisite feed, went to the officer of the day, Lieutenant Plant, and complained, but the

17

Lieutenant, perceiving his condition, paid little attention to him, upon which Hogan went to the tent where the oats were kept, and filled his horses' nose-bags. The Lieutenant caught him in the act, and while trying to empty the bags, Hogan struck him. Plant called the guard which Hogan also resisted, but in the end he was tied up by the thumbs so that his toes just touched the ground. After a little he began to make a great outcry as best he could with a gag in his mouth; when some members of the 36th and 44th Illinois Reg'ts, passing that way, heard him and saw how he was situated. They immediately went to Captain Barnett and demanded his release, but the Captain told them that they could mind their own business, and he could manage his battery without their help. The infantrymen went to their regiments and reported the case, when two or three hundred returned to the battery and made the same demand saying, if Barnett did not release Hogan, they would. The Captain told them that the first man that laid hands on the prisoner he would put a bullet through him. Then the infantrymen ran and got their guns and returned to the fence outside the camp, declaring the man should be taken down or they would put daylight through the Captain. Barnett then ordered up two cannons and had them double shotted with cannister, then told the infantrymen that the first attempt made to release Hogan would end in the slaughter of all who tried it. At this instant, while destruction seemed to threaten both parties, Colonel Knobelsdorf [Charles Knoblesdorff], of the 44th Reg't, appeared on the scene, and demanded the release of the prisoner, to which Captain Barnett consented, providing the Colonel would take him in charge, which Knoblesdorff agreed to do. The infantrymen departed with the prisoner, jeering the Captain and cheering the Colonel, but the end was not yet. The case was reported to [Major] General Rosencranz [William S. Rosecrans], com-

6. Colonel Charles Knoblesdorff, of Chicago, commanding the 44th Illinois Infantry, was tried at a general court martial on two charges: "Disobedience of orders" and "conduct unbecoming an officer and gentleman." The Hogan incident was the basis for the second charge. Colonel Knoblesdorff pleaded not guilty to all charges but was convicted and was dismissed from the service of the United States on August 15, 1862. There is a note on the 44th Illinois muster roll in the Illinois State Archives, Springfield, "Disability removed December 31, 1863."—See General Orders, No. 76, District of West Tennessee, Aug. 20, 1862.

manding the department, who ordered Knoblesdorff and Hogan to be court-martialed. Colonel Knoblesdorff was dismissed the service in disgrace,[6] and Hogan was sentenced to work with ball and chain on the breastworks at Corinth. He never returned to the battery.

Rations of whiskey had been issued to the men of the battery since the beginning of the siege of Corinth, but at this time an order from General Asboth had discontinued the use of intoxicating beverages among the troops. Of course the men missed their usual stimulant and made complaint to the officers who turned the matter over to Brown, the quartermaster sergeant, who went to headquarters and so represented the condition of Battery I to General Asboth, showing the absolute necessity of its use in that organization in order to save it from destruction by malaria, that the general melted and signed Brown's requisition, but stipulated that every dose should have a generous portion of Quinine. That drug being scarce and costly, the most of the whiskey the men got was unadulterated. One thing noticeable connected with this event was that during the summer while the battery stayed at Rienzi, the astonishing number of officers from different regiments, who were afflicted with malarial complaints that demanded daily calls on Captain Barnett. The "dry goods" labeled "Quinine" remained like the "Widow's cruse," but the "wet goods" labeled "Old Rye" replenished not, but became a thing of the past, though many an officer felt its revivifying spirit and departed with a satisfied glow of health upon his brow.

July 1st the battery, with Companies B and C of the 66th Ills. Vol., were ordered to report to General Sheridan [7] at Booneville, he having been attacked by General [James L.] Chalmers, commanding a force of one thousand cavalry, but Sheridan was too much for the Southerner, even with his small force of less than a thousand.[8]

7. For part of the summer of 1862, Battery I served in the 5th Division, commanded by Brigadier General Gordon Granger, of the Army of the Mississippi, commanded by Brigadier General William S. Rosecrans.
8. Sheridan reported that he had a total of 837 officers and men engaged with more than 5,000 confederate cavalry. This engagement added greatly to the young colonel's reputation, and from this time on, he was marked as one destined to achieve high rank. Indeed, his promotion to Brigadier General was to date from the Battle of Booneville.—See *Sheridan*, Vol. 1, pp. 156–65.

When the reinforcement reached Booneville the fight was over, so the battery returned to camp at Rienzi the same day.

While in camp at Rienzi during the summer of '62, the men suffered very much from heat, for during the months of June and July the thermometer often stood as high as 125° to 130° in the sun, the heat being so intense that all mounted drills were made early in the morning at daybreak, so the men and horses would not suffer from the high temperature. Many were without shoes, so by drilling early the hot sands were kept from blistering their feet. One of the men was sick with jaundice, and also his feet were very sore. An old colored woman seeing his condition, took pity on him and gave him the only pair of shoes she had, and would not accept any recompense, saying, all she asked, was a promise, that if he ever found one of her race in need of help, he would return the kindness. The promise was given and faithfully executed.

One day the battery was ordered out on inspection, when it was expected that every man would appear with a clean uniform and shoes polished to perfection. Ike [Isaac W.] Jones (now deceased), possessing no shoes, but wishing to show off to the best advantage, blacked his feet to the ankles. The inspector passed along the line till he came to where Ike was standing, when he halted, looked at Ike's feet, and then looked him over from head to foot, and with a quizzical expression he asked, "Well done; where did you get your blacking?" "From the bottom of my campkettle, sir," was the reply.

A building near the camp was taken possession of and turned into a hospital for the sick of the battery. Bunks were fitted up the best that could be done, and everything was made as comfortable as possible, and a placard put up over the door with the inscription, "Battery I, Hospital No. 1." A contract surgeon, Harold Hart, had charge of it, and of whom much was said, pro and con, in regard to his care of the afflicted. One story ran like this. At one time he drew by requisition twelve bottles of wine for the purpose of making bitters for the sick boys. He represented that they needed a good bitter wine tonic. A bottle of wine was so well diluted that it made four quarts of "Quinine tonic," as he named it; the other eleven bottles were laid away for a "wet day," when more tonic should be needed for the "stomach's sake." He was a strong temperance reformer of whom the boys were a little suspicious of always taking his wine straight. Every bunk had a bottle of this "tonic" with a spoon beside, placed at its head, with direction to take a spoonful every two hours without exception, unless asleep or dead, which was faithfully carried out, barring that that was poured down the rat holes in the floor. Jaundice, rheumatism, sunstroke, fevers of all kinds were dosed from the all healing "tonic" flavored with the one precious bottle of Port wine.

August 27th a squadron of rebel cavalry made a dash into the camp of Sheridan's cavalry, just south of the camp of Battery I, which roused the whole camp for a short time; but the 1st Kansas Reg't of cavalry soon drove them away, and at Newland's Store on the Ripley road, dispersed the whole of their command under Colonel [W. W.] Faulkner. It was an unlooked for event, and for a time gave the boys plenty to talk about over their campfires.

ORDERS HAD already been given to the battery to be ready to march at a moment's notice, so when the order came to move, September 6th, all were prepared to pack their traps and get ready to move. The "Pea Ridge Brigade," consisting of the 36th Illinois, 44th Illinois, 2nd Missouri and 15th Missouri Reg'ts, with Hescock's battery, and Battery I were selected by General Grant to go north and reinforce the fresh levies of troops that were being made to head off the rebel forces under [Major] General [Edmund] Kirby Smith and General [Braxton] Bragg, which were rapidly making their way towards Cincinnati and Louisville.

General Sheridan was given the command of the brigade, and went as far as Louisville, while the 36th Reg't and Battery I went by rail to Columbus, thence by boat to Cairo, thence by railroad via Vandalia, Ills. and Indianapolis, Ind., to Cincinnati. The men were glad to take a change from the dull routine of camp life to the more

3

THE BATTLE OF
PERRYVILLE

In which Battery I leaves Rienzi, Mississippi, and arrives at Louisville, Kentucky, to become a part of the force that will oppose General Braxton Bragg's "Invasion of Kentucky." Battery I, now a part of Brigadier General Philip H. Sheridan's 11th Division of the Army of the Ohio, and in Colonel Daniel McCook's 36th Brigade, left Louisville and on October 8, 1862 played an important role in the Battle of Perryville (or Chaplin Hills). Following the futile pursuit of Bragg after the battle, the Battery arrives at Nashville, Tennessee on November 7, where it remained doing garrison duty until August of 1863.

active movements of a campaign, though there was a sense of sadness, as of one leaving home, when the last lingering look was taken of the old camp at Rienzi. On the march to Corinth to take the cars, through a misunderstanding, Sergeant Rufus Stolp was reduced to the ranks; but he, notwithstanding the injustice with which he was treated, always proved himself to be one of the best of men and soldiers, serving to the end of the war, returning to make one of the best of American citizens. The trip to Columbus was made in freight cars, in which the men were huddled like cattle. The rest of the journey on the railroad was made in decent passenger cars, and was much enjoyed by the men on account of the variety and change of scenery.[1]

From some cause while passing through Illinois, the train

1. The men of Battery I had to unload and reload their guns five times in 36 hours on this movement to Kentucky.—See *Woodruff*, p. 424.

stopped for over an hour at a small station near Vandalia. A few of the battery boys who had become disgusted with the drinking water on board the cars determined to explore the village for something more refreshing and invigorating to the inner man. They called upon one of the adopted citizens of German extraction, a large and portly man, who was the owner of a small beer saloon. He was politely asked, if he would kindly and benevolently supply them with that which cheers but does not inebriate a Dutchman, as their long journey had caused their spirits to droop, their muscles to weaken, thirst to strengthen, in fact, they had fought, bled and suffered in order to save the one great and glorious Union. There is no telling how long the soldier would have talked had not the Teutonic beer vender abruptly broken the thread of his discourse by saying: "Haf you got some monish?" The boys, not being supplied with any of Uncle Sam's legal tender, appealed to the German's patriotism. They told him that every one who sold beer, so far, along the route through the Prairie State, had willingly and gladly supplied them, trusting till thirty days after the close of the war. With a frown and a look of business importance he replied: "No, no, sir, when you got no monish, you got no beer." That settled it; and in less than five minutes every keg and bottle in the place was empty, and about seventy-five canteens were full of the "Goot lager beer." When the cars pulled into Indianapolis, from the appearance, it would seem that the spirits had risen, the muscles had strengthened, and each car had been through an active engagement at the front, while the men were going to the rear.

One sad event occurred before the train reached Indianapolis, which spread a gloom over the otherwise hilarious trip, and that was the violent death of Comrade John Miller. He would persist in riding on top of the cars, and in passing over a bridge his head came in contact with the top, crushing his skull and killing him instantly. At the first station after the accident a detail was left with the body to see that it was properly buried.

Without further incident worthy of description the battery arrived in Cincinnati, on the evening of September 12th, where was found a very much excited city. Upon its arrival the battery was received by a committee of citizens, who welcomed the old veterans and offered them the freedom of the city, giving each organization a good square meal spread in the market house, before they marched over the river into Covington. The boys were in a condition to appreciate a good breakfast, cooked in "God's country," after so long and dusty a ride. On the 15th the battery crossed into Kentucky, and camped a short distance south of Covington, beside the Licking River, where it stayed till the 19th, when Kirby Smith having retreated with the purpose of joining Bragg before Louisville, the battery was ordered to that point.

Most of the troops at Covington were transported to Louisville by the river, and their embarkation at Cincinnati made a grand spectacle. The battery, while waiting for its turn to go aboard, occupied a high bluff on the Kentucky shore, which overlooked the city on the north side, also the craft in the river, many of them already loaded with troops and anchored in the stream. It was afternoon. The western sun, with its autumn rays lighted the scene, the city with its spires and glittering roofs against the background of distant hills, banners waving, drums beating, bugles sounding, bands playing, men cheering, steam organs shrieking patriotic airs, ah, this was glorious spectacular war! Then one by one the steamers dropped down the stream and the echoing hills reigned in silence, as the boat with the battery on board brought up the rear of the river fleet.

On arriving at Louisville the battery rejoined the "Pea Ridge Brigade," which was camped up the river near the asylum for the blind, though the battery camped near the river in what is now known as Butcher's Town. From this camp the battery moved out to the line of works that were being built around the city on the south, in anticipation of an attack from General Bragg. General Sheridan was now given a division consisting of the Thirty Fifth, Thirty Sixth, and Thirty Seventh Brigades, with Battery I 2nd Illinois, and Battery G 1st Missouri, Captain Hescock. The old regiments were mingled with the new, except the brigade commanded by Colonel Daniel McCook, which consisted of the 85th, 86th, 125th Illinois Regt's, and the 52nd Ohio. Sheridan's division was in the Third

Corps, commanded by [Brigadier] General C. [Charles] C. Gilbert, in the army of the Ohio, commanded by [Major] General [Don Carlos Buell] Buel.[2]

While in front of Louisville Captain Barnett was ordered to send two non-commissioned officers to the Chief of Engineers for duty on the breastworks that were being built around the city. Sergeant McDonald and Corporal Murphy were detailed, and reported to the Engineer who assigned them to take charge of a gang of citizens (white and black) who had been drafted to help build the outworks. Murphy's gang, about thirty in number, were nearly half and half, white and black, all white being outspoken rebels, who were continually breathing out curses against the "Yankee nigger lovers," as they called the "boys in blue." The moment the Corporal's back was turned they would stop work and throw out their inuendoes and slings, till his patience was exhausted. He called up a young and bright-looking mulatto, who was working very industriously and quietly in the ditch, and putting a revolver in his hands, ordered him to see that every one kept to his work, telling him to bring the first man to him that refused to work, Murphy then went to oversee some work at the other end of the ditch. This method did away with the laggards, but the abuse of the soldiers was kept up in an undertone the rest of the day. The next day the sergeant and the corporal were ordered to report back to the battery for duty, and the same day the battery moved out of the unfinished works and camped beside

2. Sheridan had been promoted to Brigadier General to date from July 1, 1862, the date of the Battle of Booneville. On September 29, 1862, Major General Don Carlos Buell put Sheridan in command of the 11th Division of the Army of the Ohio. The Division had three Brigades, the 35th, commanded by Lt. Colonel Bernard Laiboldt; the 36th, commanded by Col. Daniel McCook; and the 37th, commanded by the former Colonel of the 36th Illinois, Nicholas Greusel. Altogether, Sheridan now commanded twelve infantry regiments (seven from Illinois) and two batteries of artillery (one from Illinois).

Battery I was transferred from the Artillery Division, Army of the Mississippi to the Artillery, Army of the Ohio, and then to the artillery of Sheridan's 11th Division, 3rd Army Corps, Army of the Ohio, in September, 1862. The Army of the Ohio, commanded by Major General Don Carlos Buell, Major General George H. Thomas, 2nd in command, was organized into 3 Army Corps on September 29, 1862. The 1st Corps, commanded by Major General Alexander McD. McCook, had 2 divisions, the 3rd, commanded by Brigadier General Lovell H. Rousseau and the

Colonel Dan McCook's Brigade (one of the celebrated fighting McCooks of Ohio), with which brigade the battery, ever after to the end of the war, marched and fought. While in this camp the battery was made a six-gun organization by the addition of two three-inch Parrots [Parrotts]. Being short handed for six guns, details were made from the different regiments in the division to make up the necessary quota.

It is to be regretted that no roster of the detailed men was kept in the battery, for they ever proved themselves the best of soldiers, and endeared themselves to both officers and the regular members of the battery.

October 1st T. C. S. Brown was promoted to Quartermaster Sergeant, in place of Haight who was promoted to Junior 2nd Lieutenant. S. J. Murphy was promoted to Sergeant and placed in charge of one of the Parrott guns. Lieutenant A. W. Coe was taken sick about this time and removed to the hospital.

General Buell having recuperated and reorganized, his army moved from Louisville[3] to attack Bragg whose main army was near Bardstown, on the 1st of October '62. Battery I was one of the marching bodies among that vast throng of nearly a hundred thousand men, and what with the new horses and new detailed men there were many laughable blunders and mishaps. The second day out from Louisville Buell's army was drawn up in line at Bardstown with the prospect of a battle with Bragg's forces. The battery was in

10th, commanded by Brigadier General James S. Jackson; the 2nd Army Corps was commanded by Major General Thomas L. Crittenden, with 3 divisions, the 4th, commanded by Brigadier General William S. Smith, the 5th by Brigadier General Horation P. Van Cleve and the 6th by Brigadier General Thomas J. Wood; the 3rd Army Corps, commanded by Major General Charles C. Gilbert, had 3 divisions, the 1st, commanded by Brigadier General Alben Schoepf, the 9th, Brigadier General Robert B. Mitchell, and the 11th, Brigadier General Philip H. Sheridan.

3. The authors do not mention one of the great sensations of the day—the death of Brigadier General William Nelson by the hand of Brigadier General Jefferson C. Davis. Apparently the two men had quarreled earlier, and when they met at the Galt House in Louisville on September 29, they quarreled again, Nelson slapped Davis' face, and then Davis shot and mortally wounded Nelson. The exact details of the argument were never discovered and Davis was not prosecuted for Nelson's death.

the line in front of the town, but all at once the rebels disappeared and a night march took the place of a battle. It was the first experience of traveling over rough and stony bypaths in a dark night through a strange country. One of the guns got wedged into a crevice between rocks, and in trying to get it out the stock of the gun was broken. It was after midnight before the battery arrived in position at a ford it was to defend on the morrow, but the morning sun shone through a hazy mist, with no enemy in view, so after an early breakfast, the battery moved on towards the coming battle of Perryville.[4]

The battery now consisted of the right section of two ten-pound James' rifled guns, commanded by Lieutenant H. B. Plant; the center section of two twelve-pound Napoleon guns, under command of Orderly Sergeant Rich; the left section of two ten-pound Parrott guns, commanded by Captain C. M. Barnett. Sergeants Charles McDonald and H. W. Hill had charge of the guns of the right section; Sergeants S. J. Murphy and Z. Miller, those of the left section. The center section was sent to the rear on the 8th, so did not take part in the battle of Perryville, as it was guarding the ammunition train.

On the 7th the battery was ordered into position on a hill, but did not stay long as it soon after took a position farther to the rear. At daylight on the morning of the 8th it was moved to the front and fired the opening gun of the hard-fought battle of Perryville, Ky., sup-

---

4. The descriptions which follow of the Battle of Perryville (or Chaplin Hills) are accurate and bear out the fact that Battery I played an important part in the struggle. Generally, as the Union troops approached Perryville, Sheridan's Division, with Battery I, was out in front. Because of a drought, water was quite scarce, and Sheridan was able to establish a position on high ground, protecting the pools of water in Doctor's Creek. The Union line ran from north to south, with McCook on the left or north, Mitchell in the center, and Crittenden on the right or south. The Confederate attack, hit the Union left, pushing McCook back and exploiting the point where McCook and Crittenden met. This attack was finally stopped, partially by Sheridan's artillery delivering a flanking fire on the attackers. Then an attack hit Sheridan's position, and again the artillery played a significant role in its repulse. Then a Union counterattack pushed the Confederates from the field and out of Perryville. For those who wish to study this battle, Sheridan's *Memoirs*, I, 193–201, and his report in U.S. War Department (compiler), *The War of the Rebellion: A compilation of the Official Records of the Union and Con-*

ported by the Thirty Sixth and Thirty Seventh Brigades of Sheridan's division. Only two sections were engaged, the right and left.

In this battle the men showed their "staying qualities." From three different points the rebels opened on them, but Battery I soon silenced them; disabling one gun so that it was of no further use to the enemy. The battery changed position four times during the day. The last position was on a hill, fronting northeast, with a cornfield in front, and the enemy in force in the woods opposite. The rebels suffered so much from the guns of the battery, that they concluded to try to capture it, and the brigade supporting it. While their guns kept up a continuous fire on the battery and infantry supporting, they formed in division and charged across the cornfield, their commander mounted on a splendid gray charger. Both rider and horse were killed, and the shells from Battery I made gaps in their columns, but they closed up their ranks, and come on until within a hundred yards of the guns, when the infantry poured into their column a raking cross fire, while the battery gave them double-shotted canister from the guns. Huge gaps were made in their columns; they wavered, broke, and retreated to the woods. It was more than they could stand, and no soldiers could stand that terrific fire from infantry and artillery at such short range. Why the Union infantry did not take advantage of their confusion and make a countercharge has always remained a mystery to the men of the battery. It looked to them as though the rebel division might have been captured.

federate Armies, 70 vols. in 28 parts (Washington, D.C.; Government Printing Office, 1880–1901), Vol. 16, Part I, pp. 1081–82. This work will be cited hereafter as O. R., followed by the series, volume, part number—if any—and the page number. The report of Lt. Colonel D. T. Cowen of the 52nd Ohio—O.R., Series I, Vol. 16, Part 1, pp. 1085–86—is of interest, as is part of the Buell Court of Inquiry, O. R., Series I, Vol. 16, Part 1, pp. 236–41. See also Robert V. Johnson and Clarence C. Buel, eds., Battles and Leaders of the Civil War, 4 vols. (New York: Century, 1887–88), Vol. 3, pp. 1–61. This work will be cited hereafter as B. & L., followed by the volume number and page. J. R. Kinnear, History of the Eighty-Sixth Regiment, Illinois Volunteer Infantry (Chicago: Tribune Company Book and Job Printing Office, 1865), pp. 12–13, hereafter cited as 86th Illinois, mentions the battery, as does L. G. Bennett and William M. Haigh, History of the Thirty-Sixth Regiment Illinois Volunteers (Aurora, Illinois: Knickerbocker & Hodder, 1876), pp. 246–75. This work cited hereafter as 36th Illinois.

BEHIND THE GUNS

Had Battery I faltered for a moment at the time the rebels made their charge it would have caused a break in Gilbert's right as disasterous as the terrible gap in [Major General Alexander McD.] McCook's corps on the left. Not a man moved from his position at the guns; not one faltered. Officers and men vied with each other in resisting the charge. Officers in the infantry regiments told Captain Barnett, after the fight was over that the stand made by the battery during the charge caused the infantry regiments to rally to the support of the battery, and thus save the day on the right of the line.

When the order was given by Captain Barnett to change position to the right, covering the cornfield, Sergeant Murphy mounted his horse, and as he gave the command, "limber to the rear," a minnie ball passed over his shoulder and tore a hole through his horse's right ear.

Not until darkness drew a veil over the terrible scene did the battle close, when all was silent save the groans of the wounded and the pitiful moans of the dying. Over this scene of carnage let us drop the curtain.

On this battle field the men of the battery proved themselves heroes. They went into action at daylight without breakfast, and fought all day without food or water.

At one time Bugler W. G. Putney gathered up the canteens of the men and started for water at a spring near by with the intention of filling them for the men so they could quench their thirst, but the "best laid plans of men and mice aft gang aglee," as the rebels had possession of the spring, and came near "gobbling up" our brave bugler. Out of twenty-seven canteens, he took with him he returned with one, and that *one empty*. He told the boys of the narrow escape he had of being captured, and they were thankful that he had returned safe, minus the "sparkling water" they were in so much need of.

The men were too tired to cook any supper, and taking the tarpaulins off of the guns, spread them on the ground, preparatory to bivouacing on the battlefield, but right here is where "fraternity, charity, and loyalty" made itself manifest. The infantry boys called them up and spread before them a bountiful supply of baked beans, hot coffee, and hard tack, to which the boys did full justice. With many hearty thanks to the infantry boys, they wrapped themselves in their blankets and were soon in the "land of nod," dreaming,

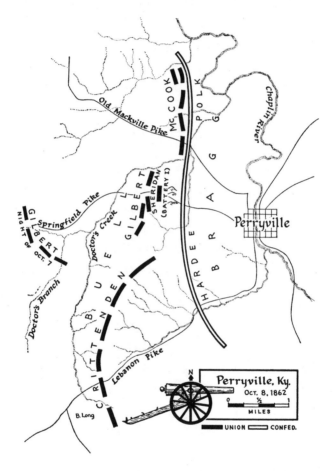

perhaps, of the dear ones at home. The only causualties in the battery were four men wounded, but none mortally.[5]

The morning of the ninth dawned brightly on the battlefield where lay the dead and wounded, as many of the wounded were not removed until morning. On the left, in front of McCook's corps, the dead were very thick in many places. [Brigadier] Generals

5. *Woodruff*, p. 425, adds: "and four men deafened." The official casualty report for the Battle of Perryville shows Battery I· had three men wounded.—See: *O. R.*, Series I, Vol. 16, Part 1, p. 1036.

[William R.] Terrill and [James S.] Jackson of the Union forces were killed, and their brigades literally cut to pieces. The ground was strewn with dead artillery horses and broken limbers and caisons, with ammunition scattered over the field. Battery I gathered up more shot, shell and canister from the field than was expended during the battle.

What must be thought of General Buell, commanding that great army, who lay in camp six miles to the rear, and who in response to General McCook's appeal for reinforcements, and that he was out of ammunition, and could only resist with bayonets, said that he "did not think that Bragg was attacking in force." Brave men were sacrificed, because the general commanding was not at the front, when he should have been, and who considered he knew more about the fighting going on, than the generals at the front in the thick of the fray. Thousands of privates in that army considered Buell as a traitor to the cause of the Union.[6]

When orders were received to pursue Bragg and his rebel hosts, who had retreated during the night, the boys fell into line with a will, and were ready to meet the enemy and fight him till the Union was restored, "one and inseparable." As the men marched by the brigade, three rousing cheers were given for Battery I, which were acknowledged by the battery boys by the lifting of hats.

The following description of the battle of Perryville was written by Dr. W. G. Putney, who served as bugler in Battery I, from June, '62, to May, '65. He was one of the first to join in '61, and was mustered out of the service at Savannah, Ga., where he had spent the last five months in the hospital, from which he was discharged disabled for further military duty.

> The roads had been very dusty and the weather very warm. The new regiments in the command discovered that the amount of clothing and other extras they were carrying on

6. Buell was not aware a major battle was in progress until late in the afternoon; the hills and general configuration of the land prevented the noise of battle from reaching his headquarters, and his contact with the troops was not all that it should have been. One computation shows that of Buell's 24 available Brigades only 9 were engaged. Had Buell concentrated his troops, it appears he could have won a major victory. The casualties were about 4,200 Union and 3,300 Confederate, killed,

backs fresh from farms and workshops, was more burden-some than they could bear. Very many well-rounded knap-sacks were unpacked by the wayside and repacked with the greatest economy of space and substance. The consequence was that many an artilleryman who had a chance to pack things away in ammunition wagons, picked up articles of clothing that came very convenient during the frosty nights that followed the battle of Perryville.

Wilbur F. Hinman in his book entitled *Si Klegg*,[7] thus humorously describes the situation as follows:

The single hour's experience on the road had served to remove the scales from the eyes of a goodly number of the members in Company Q. They began to foresee the inevita-ble, and at the first halt they made a small beginning in the labor of getting themselves down to light marching order—a process of sacrifice which a year later had ac-complished its perfect work, when each man took nothing in the way of baggage save what he could roll up in a blanket and toss over his shoulder. It was but a small beginning. They "yanked" open their knapsacks and flung away a book or an album, or an extra garment, choosing such articles as could best be spared. The sacrifice was not made without a twinge of regret, for all had their cherished keepsakes—affection's gods, that they well nigh worshipped for the sake of the loving hands that fashioned them. . . .

At the call the soldiers fell in and resumed the march. Si was quick to obey, feeling greatly refreshed by his five minutes of rest. He started off very courageously, whistling "Columbia, the Gem of the Ocean," and keeping time to the music. But he did not whistle a great while. He did not feel like it, much as he tried to make himself think he did. Hotter and hotter beat down the sun's rays as it mounted to the zenith. In streams more copious flowed the perspiration that oozed from every pore. The air was thick with dust from the countless feet of the men and horses that had gone

wounded and missing. It is possibly unnecessary to say that the lost op-portunity at Perryville was a result of a lack of information and poor administration. Buell's loyalty is beyond question.

7. Wilbur F. Hinman, *Corporal S. Klegg and his "pard." How they Lived and Talked, and what they Did and Suffered, while Fighting for the Flag* (Cleveland, Ohio: N. G. Hamilton & Co., 1892). See pp. 158–163.

before. It gathered upon Si's face; it permeated his clothes and was ground into the skin under the straps and belts that bound him. At every step his knapsack grew heavier. His heated, sweating back smarted under the pressure. Lower down his cartridge-box, with its leaden load, bobbed up and down with every footfall, chafing and grinding until that particular spot felt as if in contact with a red hot iron. His canteen and haversack rubbed the skin off his hips; the bunches of cartridges in his pocket scraped his legs; and his musket lay like a section of railroad iron upon his shoulder.

Then a new trouble came to Si, as though he had not enough already. He was young and tender—a sort of "spring chicken," so to speak. There was a sharp, smarting sensation at different points on his feet; it did not take long to blister such soft feet as he had. He felt as if somebody had poured scalding water on them, and was rubbing on salt and pepper and horse-radish, varying the treatment by thrusting in a dozen needles. What a keen, maddening pain it was! How it thrilled every nerve, as the rough shoes tore off the tender skin; and the great load of knapsack and cartridge-box and gun pressing the needles farther in at every step!

There are not many things in this world of sorrow more utterly and wildly exasperating than tramping with blistered feet on a hot day, carrying a big knapsack. A blister is not always as large as a barn-door, but for stirring up all the latent depravity of a boy's heart, it has few successful rivals.

Si began to limp, and, in spite of his efforts to prevent it, an expression of pain now and then escaped his lips. Still he kept up in his place, strong in his determination not to straggle. His efforts may have been somewhat stimulated by a blood-curdling rumor, which started at one end of the regiment and quickly ran its entire length, that a body of rebel cavalry was following leisurely along at the tail of the column, massacring all the stragglers. But the tax he had imposed upon his physical forces was too great. The spirit indeed was willing but the flesh was weak. . . .

Si's blistered feet and aching limbs and smarting shoulders told him even more plainly than his comrade's words, that the sacrifice was inevitable. He first tossed his hatchet over the fence. Then his clothes-brush and shoe-brush went; true they did not weigh much, but every ounce would help.

His frying-pan and coffee-pot he decided to be necessities. Opening his knapsack he held a melancholy inquest upon its contents. The hymn-book he speedily disposed of without carrying out his intentions of bestowing it upon a wicked cavalryman. The "Pilgrim's Progress" quickly followed. It was as much as he could do to look after his own progress as a pilgrim. He threw away the cakes of fancy soap and his sister's pincushion, after sticking half a dozen pins in his blouse. He discarded the photograph album, first taking out the pictures and putting them in his pocket. Some of the nice articles of clothing he flung upon the ground. As the weather was then he did not feel that he would ever want them. He looked at his big roll of blankets and decided that an advantageous reduction could there be made. His first plan was to abandon his blankets and keep the pretty quilt he had brought from home . . . it was settled that the broad expanse of beautiful patchwork, on which his mother had spent so many hours of toil, would have to go.

People who lived along the line of march followed the moving army for miles, gathering up the things that the new soldiers threw away. Men, women and children loaded themselves with quilts, clothing and articles of every description. . . . The shrinkage of the knapsack was the first symptom of the transformation that changed the raw recruit into an effective soldier.

Rumors of an expected battle had followed all the way from Louisville. On the 7th the battery marched in the dust and sun, and at night camped at the right of the Springfield pike, on a hill, west of Doctor's Fork [or Creek], a stream nearly dry, but with occasional pools where one, with a spoon, could dip water enough into a canteen to keep down thirst yet possessing sand and mud enough to pave the throats of those who drank. It was a cool moonlight night, and many a poor boy looked at that pale moon for the last time, as he lay under his blanket with the sky above and the earth for a bed.

At three o'clock in the morning Lieutenant Plant went round to the different guns and roused the men beside their guns and horses. The battery had stood in line of battle all night ready to move at a moment's notice. Not much breakfast was eaten, and soon the battery moved out on the pike before it was hardly light enough to see. McCook's Brigade led the way, and in a short time, from the front, came the sharp crack of the musket, sounding on the early morning air. A quiet order of halt was given to the battery, while the brave infantrymen cleared the way. Then forward again to a hill beyond just barely lighted by the coming dawn. This hill became famous as the northern name for the coming battle, Chaplin's Hill.

There was a quick move by the line of skirmishers, a short sputter or two of musketry, and with a dash the ridge was ours. By early daylight the right section under Lieutenant Plant moved up and took position on its crest, at the right of the Springfield pike. From this outlook could be seen another range of hills in the distant east. Soon a horseman on a white horse was noticed moving to and fro. Here was a living target for a shell. A gun was carefully aimed and fired, and, immediately a thousand echoes announced to many thousand listeners that the first gun of the battle of Perryville had spoken from its brazen throat the orders of the day. The rider disappeared, but in his stead came a battery to give trial of mettle for metal and shell for shell. An artillery duel followed, but if the aim of Battery I was no better than theirs no one was hurt, though many were somewhat scared, for a number of soldiers were under artillery fire for the first time, though we stayed in the same location, while they limbered several times to different positions.

The forenoon wore on. There was enough of movement in front to keep up an intense interest, and occasionally complimentary explosives were exchanged, while the angry sputter of musketry between skirmish lines gave all to understand more grave work was to be expected later. In the meantime Captain Barnett, with his section, had occupied the crest on the left of the pike. The Thirty Fifth Brigade had moved up and advanced to the front on the left of the pike; and a little later the 2nd and 15th Missouri Regiments made a charge, sweeping every thing in their front back towards Perryville, to beyond a large spring which, though it had plenty of good water, was very dangerous to approach, as it was between the lines. Later a body of cavalry occupied the cornfield to the left of the pike, but did very little fighting.

Once during the forenoon Captain Barnett taking one of the sections, dashed forward some two hundred yards towards the rebel line, poured in case shot and canister, making it lively for the enemy's line of skirmishers. After a very hot fusilade the section returned to its first position. The battery occasionally threw shells at whatever might be seen, while the enemy in front were maneuvering for a position from which to charge later in the day.

The First Brigade commanded by Brigadier General St. John [R.] Liddel, 3rd Division, [Major General William J.] Hardee's Corps, was the rebel force in front of the battery in the morning. The 5th and 7th Arkansas were the regiments driven away from the ridge by the 2nd and 15th Missouri. None were wounded or killed in the battery during the forenoon. There was a lull about noon, and the men ate of what they had, which was very little, as orders had been issued from corps headquarters that no provision trains should be allowed near the front. There was no water for the horses, and but little for the men only as it could be dipped from pools with spoons.

The roar of battle had been heard off to the left for some time, but, about half past three o'clock, a Union force was seen moving in on the left of Sheridan's Division, which proved to be the right of McCook's corps. Soon they were furiously attacked and began to give away, when both Battery I and Hescock's battery were ordered to the left of the pike, where they opened with a storm of case shot and shell, which had the effect of stopping the rebel onset in that direction for awhile. Soon the position to the right of the pike needed attention. [Major] General [Simon B.] Buckner's Division had arrived at Perryville, and he was preparing to charge Sheridan. Both batteries were now ordered to the right of the pike where, supported by all the infantry of Sheridan's division, they were to stem the furious onslaught of the desperate foe. The shell of the rebel batteries began to plow their way into the lines, while ours returned as good as was sent.

See, their line of battle has started! No more attention is paid to their batteries. Case shot and shell burst before and and in their ranks, but with their banners proudly waving, on they come, faster and faster, closing their torn ranks with a cheer that seems "to wake the hills from their eternal slumbers." Now the deadly fire of the infantry opens on them, but not to stay their progress. They have reached the cornfield and still they come. They are at the fence that bounds the field. Thank God! They have stopped for no man can climb that fence and live. Ah, the window of death is fast forming, for thousands of death-dealing missiles are flying there. What is this! Their right is swinging around so as to enfilade our left, which is producing some confusion in the line, but only for a moment. The tempest of our fire is turned that way and the danger is over. The 36th Illinois is out of ammunition and must retire, which some take to be a retreat, but again through the bravery of the officers and the valor of the batteries the flurry is soon stayed, and the battle goes on.[8] The rebels are beginning to drop back from the fence, first in squads then in companies, finally all have gone that care to go and the charge has been gloriously stayed. There is a lull, then over on the right of McCook's corps the battle is on more furious than ever. Again the batteries return to the left of the pike, and again by their overwhelming fire are the rebel hosts driven back.

But all things must cease for time waits not for the acts of man. The sun is getting low in the west and the warring hosts have exhausted their fiery zeal. The oncoming darkness casts its shadows before on the minds of men, cooling their hate and urging to rest. After such a deafening and infernal roar of battle silence seems unnatural and solemn, while the hush is made painful by the presence of death and destruction, seen and heard in the groans of the wounded and the low moans of the dying.

The ammunition wagons are brought up from the rear to replenish the empty limber chests. The ambulances come for the wounded. The surgeons are busy with lint and bandages, chloroform and knife, while nurses bear the wounded in and the maimed out to the tents or rudely constructed shelters. Campfires are built and men gather round them to tell the incidents of the day. Some have little to eat, which they share with their comrades, and a small quantity has been smuggled to the front in the ambulances and ammunition wagons. Soon

8. According to the report of Captain Silas Miller commanding the 36th Illinois, to Colonel N. Greusel, commanding the 37th Brigade: "Finding the ammunition running low, adjutant Beddulph was sent for more, but it becoming entirely consumed before his return and the enemy's fire much slackened, the regiment was ordered to 'fix bayonets'; but being advised by you that the enemy's cavalry menaced us towards the left, the regiment was ordered 'by the right of companies to the rear,' leaving

the joke and the laugh goes round, and so with the warm coffee the spirits rise and the bright side shows itself.

At night while the bugler was filling canteens with a spoon, several of the infantrymen were occupied in like manner, when one of them noticing his uniform, inquired what battery, and was told Battery I. "Well, sir," says the infantryman, "All the men in that battery ought to be made commissioned officers for the way they stood by their guns, this afternoon."

After the charge had spent its force, there was a lull of battle roar and the wounded began to pass in rear of the battery, some hobbling, some borne on stretchers, some assisted by comrades. The rebel batteries were still throwing shell at our line, the most of which passed over and burst in the rear among the ambulances and wounded. On one of the stretchers was a wounded man who made a great outcry of distress. The sympathies of all that heard him were intensely aroused. Suddenly a shell burst close by which so demoralized the men carrying him that they dropped the stretcher and ran to the rear as fast as their legs could carry them. The wounded man's outcries ceased. He raised himself on his elbow and, for an instant, looked around him, then jumping to his feet he ran after those that had been bearing him, and soon outstripped them in their race for safety. Of course the sympathizers cheered and laughed, while the procession of wounded continued to pass with their blood-stained forms writhing in pain from their terrible, mangled, agonizing wounds.

There were no men killed nor horses badly wounded or killed, which to one present, seems almost miraculous, for bullets seemed to hail into the battery, and can only be accounted for, by the fact, that the rebel line at the foot of the ridge either fired into the side, or high above it; and one other thing, the infantry and batteries' fire was so overwhelming that their fire was kept down and very much confused.

By daylight, the 9th, all was ready for renewal of battle or an advance. Soon it was discovered that the "Johnies" had

space for another regiment (the 24th Wisconsin), supplied with ammunition. Some confusion was occasioned in returning, on account of the 88th Illinois covering the three right companies, but after passing through the battery, a new line was promptly formed to the left of the battery, on the left of the road, in the cornfield, where our ammunition was immediately replenished."—*36th Illinois*, p. 283.

retired from the front, and the battle of Perryville, barren of result, was a thing of the past to be known only in history. The battery moved towards Perryville and got some of that cool sweet spring water that had been so longed for the day before, but could not be obtained, because rebel lead searched the ground and held its pure waters from parched lips. At night the battery camped east of Chaplin River, and the next day, being rainy, it lay in camp, while a number of men was sent to search the ground fought over, for horses let loose during the fight by the casualties of battle. Oh, what evidences of carnage, and how terrible it looked! War is dreadful, but it needs must come at times to purge out great wrongs that can only be remedied by its scourge.

The 12th a short march was made towards Harodsburg [Harrodsburg], and camped at night in the rain. The 13th there was a march of a mile or two, showing the dilatory tactics of General Buell in following General Bragg. The 14th the march was longer and through a most beautiful country, passing Danville. In the afternoon, of which William M. Haigh, Chaplain of the 36th Illinois, says in his history: [9] "This is one of the finest towns in Kentucky, in the blue grass region. The houses were attractive, the gardens and grounds laid out with great taste and planted with evergreens. But the brightest recollection of Danville is connected with the Ladies' Seminary, at the windows of which stood crowds of young ladies, whose variety of beautiful dresses gave them the appearance of bouquets of flowers, and whose loyalty was expressed by the waving of handkerchiefs and flags. Most heartily did the boys respond to their greeting."

That night the battery camped near the town of Lancaster, and in the morning which was frosty, the battery moved through the town amidst cheering and waving of flags, regimental bands playing, everything having the appearance more of a holiday than the time of grim-visaged war. In the distance was the booming of

9. *Ibid.*, p. 294.

10. Woodruff says it was the 16th when Battery I reached Crab Orchard.— *Woodruff*, p. 425.

11. Major General William Starke Rosecrans replaced General Buell because of widespread public dissatisfaction with Buell following the es-

cannon and the rattle of musketry as our vanguard was pursuing the rebel rearguard. The people in this section seemed to be mostly loyal, at least they showed that way. Again we witnessed the glory of war in the spectacular form.

That night the division reached Crab Orchard [10] and camped there till the 21st, having closed the campaign in Kentucky against Bragg. When the army moved it started towards the north, much to the disgust and anger of the men who were already rebellious towards General Buell. Camped that night at Mitchell, and the next day on Salt River, about four miles from Lebanon Station, staying there till the 25th, which day's march was very disagreeable from cold, at first rain, then snow, in which the battery went into camp at Newmarket. The next morning the boys found themselves wading in five inches of snow. The men were ill prepared for winter weather, being without shoes and tents, consequently there was much suffering among the infantrymen. The 27th the army started for Bowling Green during which march the battery camped within seven miles of Mammoth Cave, which Captain Barnett with a few others visited.

November 1st the division camped at Bowling Green, where General Rosecrans joined the army, having been given the command of the Army of the Ohio in place of General Buell.[11] November 4th the troops started for Nashville.

Late in the afternoon, on the 7th, after four days march over rough roads and hilly country, the battery arrived at Edgefield, a suburban town, on the north side of Cumberland River, opposite Nashville. Remained in this camp for a short time during which General Rosecrans reviewed the whole army. The change in commanders was very acceptable to the rank and file, and Rosecrans soon became very popular with the army.

The next move was to College Hill in Nashville,[12] and from there to Mill Creek, six miles south of Nashville, on the Nolensville pike, where the division remained in camp for over three weeks. Thanks-

cape of the confederate army after the relatively unproductive Battle of Perryville.

12. Woodruff says Battery I reached Nashville on November 1 and Mill Creek on the 22nd.—*Woodruff*, p. 425.

giving Day, the Battery and the [2nd and] 15th Missouri, 44th, 88th, and 36th Illinois, went out a foraging towards Nolensville, about six miles. They drove in the rebel cavalry pickets, with which there was quite a sharp skirmish. Most of the boys brought back something to eat, drink, or smoke, having found a barn stored with plenty of tobacco. For a few days there was an extensive traffic in the filthy weed. While in this camp the renowned "pup tent" made its first appearance, much to the disgust of the soldiers who declared that Uncle Sam wanted to make "dogs" out of free American citizens. John A. Kelly was discharged at this time from the battery, to accept a commission as lieutenant in the 100th Illinois infantry. December 10th the battery was relieved from duty in Sheridan's division and attached to Colonel McCook's brigade, which was placed in the Reserve Corps, commanded by [Major] General Gorden [Gordon] Granger,[13] and assigned to garrison duty in Nashville. The brigade commanded by Colonel G. W. Roberts, of the 42nd Illinois, which had been doing garrison duty, and Battery C. 1st Illinois, commanded by Captain Charles Houghtailing [Houghtaling], were ordered to General Sheridan's division. Upon reporting to [Brigadier] General [Robert B.] Mitchell, commanding the garrison forces, Captain Barnett was appointed Chief of Artillery and Inspector of Horses for Nashville.

The Army of the Ohio moved on the 26th to attack General Bragg's forces at Murfreesboro. The battle began early on the

13. General Rosecrans reorganized the Army, and the Army and Department of the Cumberland was born and organized into the 14th Army Corps, which had a Right Wing, a Centre and a Left Wing. Major General Alexander McD. McCook commanded the Right, Major General George H. Thomas the Centre, and Major General Thomas L. Crittenden the Left. These designations would be changed on January 9, 1863, to 14th, 20th and 21st Army Corps.

Battery I had been in the Army of the Ohio (commanded by General Buell), 3rd Corps (commanded by General Gilbert), 11th Division (commanded by General Sheridan). With Rosecrans reorganization, Sheridan's Division became the 3rd Division of the Right wing; Colonel G. W. Roberts Brigade, which included Battery C, 1st Illinois Light Artillery, had been the 1st Brigade, 13th Division, Army of the Ohio, and now became the 3rd Brigade of Sheridan's Division. General Robert B. Mitchell had commanded the 1st Division of the Right wing but on November 5 was transferred to command the 4th Division of the Centre. Battery I went from Sheridan's command to Mitchell's 4th Division—

morning of the 31st, 1862, and lasted till the 3rd of January, 1863. The first day's fight was disastrous to the Union army, but the last was a defeat to the rebels, which ended in the occupation of Murfreesboro and the retreat of Bragg's army to Tullahoma.[14]

The encampment of the battery was on the Grannywhite pike, about forty rods north of the toll gate, on a hill west and in the same range as was Fort Negley. There was a large brick house, once occupied by the master, while the brick Negro quarters were in the same yard. The place had been the residence of some wealthy retired planter. Now, in the year 1896, there is a bare rocky surface, with free Negro cabins on all sides. The old drill ground west of the pike is now covered with suburban residences.

During the winter of '62 and '63, nothing of importance occurred in and around Nashville. After the battle of Stone River Rosecrans was gradually getting the Army of the Cumberland in hand and gathering rations, forage, and ammunition, making Nashville his base of supplies, so as to be ready to move as soon as the rainy season was over. The men were drilled daily, whenever the weather would permit, and it was not long before it was considered one of the best drilled batteries in the army.

For awhile the boys enjoyed garrison duty, and with an occasional scouting and foraging expedition, they managed to pass away the time very pleasantly, but garrison life soon grew tiresome, and they longed for the march, with its daily change of camp life, and

of which Daniel McCook commanded the 2nd Brigade—in November.

In January, 1863, the Battery was again transferred, this time to the artillery of Brigadier General James D. Morgan's 4th Division of the 14th Army Corps (Major General George H. Thomas) of the Army of the Cumberland. In June, 1863, the Battery was transferred to the Reserve Corps, commanded by Major General Gordon Granger, 2nd Division, commanded by General Morgan. It was attached to the 2nd Brigade of this Division; the units were the old friends of the Battery, the 85th, 86th and 125th Illinois and the 52nd Ohio, commanded by Col. Daniel McCook.

14. General Bragg was successful on December 31 in forcing the Union forces back, although he did not drive them from the field. The confederate attack on January 2, 1863, was a failure, and losses were heavy. On the evening of January 3, Bragg began to withdraw towards Tullahoma. The battle, initially a success for the confederates, ended in their withdrawal, and overall, must be considered a strategic failure.

wished they were at the front. The men thought, and no doubt it was true, there was too much unnecessary discipline for volunteers, and some of the men were continually undergoing some kind of punishment.

In February Lieutenant Haight rejoined the battery from Springfield, Ills., and on the 20th sent in his resignation, which was accepted. March 23rd Lieutenant Coe rejoined the battery from the hospital, and reported for duty.

In March the battery boys, non-commissioned and commissioned officers, gave a dance, and those of the boys who "tripped the light fantastic toe" had a merry time. The only trouble was that there were more "sojer boys" than girls, and the men were the "Wall flowers" that evening. There was a good "lay out" of rations and plenty of punch, and along about dawn of the next day the ambulances conveyed the girls to their homes.

During the spring Lieutenant W. E. Hayward rejoined from recruiting service, and handed in his resignation as Senior 2nd Lieutenant. Shortly after his resignation he accepted a commission as Captain in the 2nd United States Volunteers, and was assigned to the department of the West, and served under General Pope until the close of the war.

In April Orderly Sergeant Rich was promoted to 2nd Lieutenant,[15] *vice* Haight resigned, and on the 7th of the month the boys of the battery presented him with a beautiful sword, belt, and revolver. He was so surprised at its presentation that he could only stammer out his thanks.

In the month of June the boys, to show their appreciation of Comrade W. G. Putney, bugler of the battery, bought a bugle, and had it properly engraved, and one pleasant day it was presented to him before the whole battery. It is unnecessary to say that the brave bugler was highly pleased with the gift, and the kind words that went with the bugle, and to this day it is one of his most cherished

---

15. Barnett recommended 1st Sgt. Judson Rich for Senior 2nd Lieutenant, *vice* Hayward, in a letter dated February 10, 1863, which went through channels. Colonel Daniel McCook noted: "If we ever expect to make our army fully efficient, *promotion must be made from the ranks.* I saw the cool, determined gallantry of this sergeant, for he fought under

mementoes of the war. At the reunions of the survivors of Battery I Comrade Putney brings it with him, battered and worn, and sounds the old familiar battery calls to the delight of his comrades.

During the summer the gun squads drilled for a prize, a five-pound package of smoking tobacco; the officers to be judges, and the Captain to give the prize. The "squad" that loaded and fired, dismantled the gun and mounted it in the quickest time was to have the tobacco. The quickest time made was forty-five seconds. A majority of the officers made their decision in favor of one given squad, but the Captain favored another, and overruled their decision, and gave the tobacco to his favorite, whereupon the lieutenants bought five pounds of tobacco, and presented it to the sergeant of the squad which, they had decided, had won the prize. After that there was no more prize-drills, as they bred ill-feeling between the different squads.

An open field, in the southwest part of the city, alongside of the Grannywhite pike, was used as a drill ground for McCook's brigade and the battery. Hundreds of citizens from the city, besides the infantry soldiers would be on hand when the battery went out to drill. The men and horses became almost perfect in their drill and experienced officers of the regular army declared they never saw a better drilled battery in the regular army. For a change Colonel Dan McCook concluded to have sham battles, his infantry regiments to attack and try and capture the battery. During one of these sham attacks, Bugler Putney took Colonel Dan McCook prisoner, and was the hero for that day.

One beautiful day the men were resting after their exertions of going through a sham battle, and the drivers had dismounted. The horses of the battery had become so well acquainted with the yells of the charging infantry, that as soon as they heard the familiar sound, they were ready for the race. Colonel McCook had formed his brigade during its maneuvers into a hollow square to resist cavalry,

my eye for 14 hours at Perryville. I have watched his soldierly qualities upon the long, harrassing march from Louisville after Bragg to this place [Nashville], and know that he will do honor to the position." Brigadier General James D. Morgan also endorsed favorably Barnett's request for Rich's promotion.

then going off a distance he returned on the full run to represent the onset of a cavalry charge. Just as he had nearly reached the line of bayonets, his horse thinking the prospect was too pointed, stopped suddenly, the saddle girths parted, and McCook and saddle went on, landing on the ground in the infantry line, just missing being caught on the point of a bayonet. The whole brigade yelled. The horses heard and taking it for granted another sham fight was on hand, sprang without their drivers, to go through their usual tactics, but finding no control each team started in a different direction. The officers and mounted non-commissioned officers rode to capture the runaways, but could only do so by catching the lead teams and circling around till the three spans were stopped enough to admit the postillions to get into their saddles. One of the horses was killed and three were wounded, besides considerable damage was done to the battery, all of which was accounted for after the great battle of Chickamauga. After that incident no more sham battles took place.

About June 15th Captain Barnett made a detail of twelve men, Sergeant Murphy in command, to escort the brigade surgeon to Brentwood, about twelve miles south from Nashville, and return. Bugler Putney had charge of the commissary, packed in glass bottles. On the return trip the surgeon proposed a race, and away they went, when going at full speed, Putney's horse fell, landing his rider headforemost on the hard pike, thereby "breaking up" the commissary department. The surgeon considered it a great loss, as it was about lunch time, and so the old adage, "Make haste slowly," flitted through his mind, and he wished he had followed it. Putney and his horse were not much damaged, and was soon mounted and on the road, and the whole party arrived at Nashville about six in the evening.

June 30th the battery left Nashville with the brigade train and five companies of the 86th Illinois infantry, and camped at LaVergne for the night. The next morning at five o'clock the train moved, and arrived at Murfreesboro at three o'clock in the afternoon, where camp was made to the west of the town, with the rest of the brigade.

July 7th news was received that Vicksburg had surrendered to

Grant, and on the morning of the 8th the siege guns were fired in honor of the event. July the 18th the battery broke camp at Murfrees-boro and started on the road back to Nashville with the brigade, arriving there on the 19th, and in a few days occupied the old camp on the hill.

July 31st Lieutenant Rich received twenty days leave of absence, and returned August 13th, a few days before the battery left Nashville for the front.

For over nine months the battery had remained at Nashville on garrison duty, but it was now to leave for the front. Rosecrans advanced from the camp at Murfreesboro on the 24th of June, and on the 1st of July Tullahoma was occupied. The Union forces followed up the retreating army as far as the Tennessee River, and on the 1st of September the Army of the Cumberland began the campaign which terminated in the battle of Chickamauga and the occupation of Chattanooga.

In which Battery I participates in the advance towards Chattanooga
called the Tullahoma Campaign, and as a part of Major General Gordon
Granger's Reserve Corps, advances into northern Alabama. From
Stevenson the Battery had a hard march to Chattanooga, and then to
Rossville, Georgia, where the stage was set for the bloody battle of
Chickamauga. The Battery was inactive the first day of the battle,
September 19, but on September 20, it marched to General Thomas'
support, was engaged, and served as rear guard as the army retreated to
Chattanooga. On September 21, Lt. Coe's section was hotly engaged by
the pursuing Confederates, but repulsed their attack. In Chattanooga, the
Battery did not get as hungry as the rest of the besieged union army
because it did its own foraging. It participated in the opening of the new
supply route, the "Cracker Line," and was engaged in Sherman's attack
on Missionary Ridge and at Chickamauga Station, then marched with
the force sent to relieve Major General Ambrose E. Burnside in east
Tennessee. Returning to the Chattanooga area, many of the Battery
re-enlist, and return to Illinois for well-earned furloughs.

 For the Chickamauga campaign, covered in this chapter, the Union
army was organized as follows:
 Commander, *Major General William S. Rosecrans.*
 14th Army Corps, *Major General George H. Thomas*
  1st Division, Brig.-Gen. Absolom Baird, 2nd Division, Maj.-Gen.
  James S. Negley, 3rd Division, Brig.-Gen. John M. Brannan, 4th

4

THE BLOODY BATTLE

OF CHICKAMAUGA

Division, Maj.-Gen. Joseph J. Reynolds
20th Army Corps, *Major General Alexander McD. McCook*
    1st Division, Brig.-Gen. Jefferson C. Davis, 2nd Division, Brig.-Gen. Richard W. Johnson, 3rd Division, Maj.-Gen. Philip H. Sheridan
21st Army Corps, *Major General Thomas L. Crittenden*
    1st Division, Brig.-Gen. Thomas J. Wood, 2nd Division, Maj.-Gen. John M. Palmer, 3rd Division, Brig.-Gen. H. P. Van Cleve
Reserve Corps, *Major General Gordon Granger*
    1st Division, Brig.-Gen. James B. Steedman, 2nd Division,
Cavalry Corps, *Brig.-Gen. Robert B. Mitchell*
    1st Division, Col. Edward M. McCook, 2nd Division, Brig.-Gen. George Crook
    Battery I was in the 2nd Division of the Reserve Corps. The 2nd Division had only one brigade, called the 2nd Brigade. This Brigade was commanded by Col. Daniel McCook, and consisted of:
    85th Illinois Infantry: *Col. Caleb J. Dilworth*
    86th Illinois Infantry: *Lt. Col. D. W. Magee*
    125th Illinois Infantry: *Col. Oscar F. Harmon*
    52nd Ohio Infantry: Maj. J. T. Holmes
    69th Ohio Infantry: Lt. Col. J. H. Brigham
    Battery I, 2nd Illinois Light Artillery, Captain Charles M. Barnett.

Aᴜɢᴜsᴛ 20th, 1863, the 2nd Brigade of General Gordon Granger's Reserve Corps, Colonel Dan McCook, commanding, to which the battery was attached, left for the front, via Columbia, Tenn., Athens, and Huntsville, Ala., the 1st Brigade having preceded.

There being no cavalry attached to the brigade a detail of fifty men from the infantry and battery was made to act as scouts. The detail was mounted and scouted night and day, confiscating horses wherever they were found, and the quartermaster sergeant of the battery was foraging for the horses and men, and managed to keep the commissary department well stocked on the march. The boys had no occasion to grumble over their rations, as they had a greater variety than was issued by Uncle Sam's commissary.

Many prisoners were taken on the march through Tennessee and Northern Alabama, and some amusing incidents occurred in connection with the scouting for forage. One day, when in camp near Spring Hill [Tennessee], it was reported that a party of bushwhackers, was prowling around west of the camp. Captain Barnett mounted about fifty men belonging to the battery on the horses of the battery, and armed them with sabres and revolvers. The detachment had quite the appearance of cavalry as they marched out of camp. Scouts were sent to the front to search for the enemy. After proceeding about four miles the scouts came back and reported men in a piece of woods across an open field. Line of battle was formed, and with a whoop and a yell it charged over the open ground into the woods. There, sure enough, were the men who broke and ran as fast as their legs could carry them with the detachment tearing after them, sabre in hand, till they were corralled in a farm house the other side of the woods. The prisoners were brought forth not to be shot, but to be recognized as some of the brigade boys with their haversacks full of apples. They were badly scared, having taken the pursuing squadron for bushwhackers, and before they hardly comprehended the situation the battery boys had borrowed all of their apples. Upon returning to camp in the afternoon, behold! it was vacant. The brigade and battery had received marching orders, and what with mule teams and extra horses, one team to a gun, they had managed to pull out of camp. The scouting detachment had to double quick about four miles before it overtook the brigade.

One night the brigade camped near the town of Lynnville, [Tennessee], situated between Columbia and Pulaski. Early in the morning a party of bushwhackers fired thirteen shots at the picket post and wounded two men quite badly. Colonel Dan McCook ordered Captain Barnett to take a detachment of mounted men and go into the town and burn a house for every shot fired, selecting such as he thought were owned by rebels, and to stay until all were burned. The order was effectually executed. Among the houses destroyed was the village tavern which had a bar well stocked with liquors. A demijohn of port wine was saved from the conflagration and disposed of by the boys after the work was done. The detachment started to return to the marching column. While on the road a party of bushwhackers was discovered in the edge of a piece of woods. Fences were torn down, and the boys charged, with a yell, across an open field into the woods, swords on high, to meet the foe in death grapple, and with a dash they were upon him, only to find a large flock of geese, which dispersed with many a quack, quack, quack. The captain desired that nothing be said about the incident, but somehow, as usual, "Murder will out," and the boys had to take their quack medicine as freely as they had taken their wine.

One day when Sergeants McDonald and Murphy were out scouting, and within half a mile of Athens, Ala., Sergeant Murphy's horse became unmanageable, took the bit between his teeth, and ran away with him into the town, McDonald following rapidly. There were about fifteen rebel cavalry in the town, their horses hitched to posts around the square, and when they saw the two wild Yankees coming, they broke for their horses, cut the hitching straps, mounted, and got out of town at a lively pace, yelling as they went, "The Yankees are coming." The citizens were not much frightened, as they had been visited by Mitchell and Colonel [John B.] Turchin a year before. One old lady was quite bitter at the Yankees. She told McDonald that that "Dirty old Dutchman, Turchin, had camped his men (the 19th Illinois infantry) on her lawn, but I got revenge" she said, "I wrote to old Abe

Lincoln, and told him what a mean man the Dutchman was; that he had captured some of my friends, and sent them north to languish in prison." She guessed he had been punished, as but a short time after "Turchin and his thieves" had been ordered away. McDonald told her that Turchin had been made a general for meritorious conduct while in Alabama. She then wanted to know who commanded the Yankee forces, which were now invading her home. She was told that Colonel Dan McCook commanded the brigade. "Well, I'm glad of that" she said, "as he is a friend of my family. My son and Dan were very close friends while in college, and he spent two weeks of his vacation at my home. I'll send my youngest boy to meet the colonel, and ask him to make my house his home while in Athens." The Colonel made her house his headquarters, as requested.

One prisoner was captured in Athens, from information given by a Union-loving woman. He called himself Colonel Higginson. The loyal citizens said he was a conscript officer, and was there for the purpose of hunting up Union men and forcing them into the rebel army. He denied the charge, but was turned over to the provost marshal. It was soon rumored around camp that, through the pleadings of his hostess, the Colonel let him go his way.

On the morning of September 4th, while the battery was preparing to take the road, George Mathers, a driver, in putting on one of his boots, was stung on the top of his big toe by a scorpion. He was put into the ambulance, and attended by one of the doctors of the brigade, who prescribed whiskey as an antidote. It was of no help for him, and he died about nine in the forenoon, while the battery was on the road to Huntsville, Ala.,[1] and a detail was left behind to bury him. Colonel Dan McCook told some of the citizens, who lived around where he was buried, that, if any harm came to any of the burial detail, he would return with his brigade and burn every house within a radius of twenty miles. It is needless to say that the burial party rejoined the battery after performing the last sad duties to their dead comrade.

While at Athens a few of the men gathered some scrubby

---

1. Woodruff says the Battery arrived at Huntsville, Alabama, on September 4. — *Woodruff*, p. 426.

peaches, and one of the boys, a corporal, noted for his love of sweet things, stewed a lot of them until he had about two quarts of preserves, when the order to march was given. He had no way to carry them, and would not divide with his comrades, as was suggested. He would not throw them away, and there was only one other alternative, and that was, eat them, which he finally did. During that day's march there was one pretty sick corporal, and he often regretted that he did not act on the advice of one of his comrades and divide the preserves with the boys.

When near Huntsville, Ala., Sergeant Murphy, in command of some scouts, saw two horsemen come out of the brush in front of them, and gave chase after them. They gained rapidly, and one of the rebels surrendered, but the other one being better mounted, escaped. The prisoner who was about six feet, four inches in height, after looking at his captors, said, "Well, I'll be d— —d, if I hav'nt been captured by a lot of d— —d artillery men!" He said that the Yankee cavalry had been after him, nearly two years, but could not catch him; they would deploy, and that would give him an opportunity to escape. He wanted to know if they were not afraid he would lead them into an ambush. They said, "No," that when they got after a rebel they generally took him in, and that they had "gobbled up" several prisoners since they left Nashville. He said he was a Texas ranger, and taking off his silver mounted spurs, presented them to the sergeant as a souvenir of the occasion, and his appreciation of the generous treatment received from his captors. He was turned over to the provost marshal who paroled him.

The battery arrived at Huntsville, Ala., about nine in the evening, of the 4th of September. Huntsville is a beautiful town with a fine location, where many Southerners spent the summers, but the boys had no time to see much of it, as they were on the march early on the morning of the 5th, and marched to within two miles of Brownsville, where they went into camp at one in the afternoon. September 6th, marched fifteen miles and then camped for the night. On the 7th, after a twenty mile march over one of the worst roads yet traveled, camp was made near Bromlets. Arrived on the 8th at Stevenson, Ala., after marching fifteen miles, and found the 1st

Brigade in camp. Left Stevenson at nine in the forenoon, on the 9th, and arrived at Bridgeport, on the Tennessee River, at three in the afternoon, and went into camp. Many of the men, soon as they could get off duty, took a refreshing bath in the river, and got rid of the dust they had accumulated on the last three days march. Crossed the Tennessee River, on the 11th, and went into camp. The 12th, marched eight miles and camped near Shell Mound and Devil's Hole. The 13th, orders were received by the troops to leave all transportation wagons behind, and march to Chattanooga, where the battery arrived the same day after a forced march of twenty-five miles. The brigade with the battery was ordered to Rossville, Ga., six miles south east of Chattanooga, where both went into camp on a rise of ground near the old Ross House, not far from General Gordon Granger's headquarters, at which place the quartermaster Sergeant, with five of the baggage wagons, rejoined the battery the next day, one of the wagons having broken down and been abandoned in Lookout Valley.

General Granger had issued strict orders in regard to foraging. No one was allowed to forage, but occasionally some of the men would get outside of the lines and bring back hogs, sheep and chickens. Four men of the 1st Brigade, who had a sheep they had

2. "General Granger was a strict disciplinarian, harsh and often unreasonable. For infractions of duty or military etiquette he could cause a soldier to be tied by the thumbs or administer the lash with as little compunction as he would apply the same mode of punishment to a dog."—*36th Illinois*, p. 215.

3. The battle of Chickamauga, in which Battery I is about to be engaged was fought on September 19 and 20 a few miles south of Chattanooga, across the border in Georgia. Rosecrans pursued Bragg into the mountains, scattering his troops as they pushed through the mountains, all the way from Alpine, Georgia (McCook) to Chattanooga, Tennessee (Granger and Crittenden). Bragg's plan was to attack and defeat each column singly, but when his plans miscarried and Rosecrans tardily brought his forces together, the plan was abandoned. To assist Bragg, General James Longstreet corps from the east had been sent to Georgia in an epic railroad movement. The Confederates attacked and the fighting on September 19 was confused and indecisive. The Union line in the valley of the Chickamauga ran from north to south: Mitchell, McCook, Thomas, Crittenden and Granger. On September 20, heavy attacks hit Thomas, and when troops were moved to his assistance, through an understandable error, a gap opened on Sheridan's left, just as Longstreet attacked. His troops poured through the gap, sending a large part of the

foraged, were arrested by the guard and taken to the General's headquarters, and by the General's orders, tied up by the thumbs, and [he] was about to issue another order to have them whipped, when brave and humane [Brigadier] General Steadman [James B. Steedman], commanding the division, with the division at his back, protested against such brutality, and the men were released and returned to their regiment. General Granger was universally detested by the men of his corps, the Reserve, and if he had ordered the men whipped, there would have been a revolution in that camp, and, no doubt, the General would have answered with his life for the act.[2]

September 18th the battery, with the brigade, was ordered out to Chickamauga Creek, to burn Reed's Bridge, but did not succeed, though a brass band and an ambulance, with a few prisoners, were captured, the advance regiment having run in between two divisions of the rebels, while they were moving for positions in the next day's battle.[3] The brigade and battery camped that night not far from the bridge. On the 19th the brigade returned towards Rossville and took up a position just outside of Rossville Gap. Here the battery remained all night in readiness for any emergency.

The Reserve Corps took no part in the battle of Chickamauga on the 19th, but early on the morning of the 20th, the brigade, with the

Union army in demoralized retreat, back towards Chattanooga. But Thomas held fast, earning the nickname "The Rock of Chickamauga," and Granger rushed troops to his aid. Battery I moved south with Granger, was engaged, and then held a position to cover Thomas' retreat. They were one of the last of the Union troops to leave the field.

Much has been written about Chickamauga, but Battery I appears in a number of references. See Archibald Gracie *The Truth about Chickamauga* (Boston and New York: Houghton Mifflin Company, 1911), pp. 83, 106–10, map facing page 112, 113–14, 186–87, 402–3, 448–49. Other sources for the activity of Battery I include: "Report of Lt. Col. David W. Magee, 86th Illinois Infantry" O. R. Series I, Vol. 30, Part 2, pp. 875–77; "Report of Col. Calbe J. Dilworth, 85th Illinois Infantry, O. R., Series I, Vol. 30, Part 1, pp. 872–74; "Report of Col. Oscar F. Harmon, 125th Illinois Infantry," O. R., Series I, Vol. 30, Part 1, pp. 878–79 and the "Report of Major James T. Holmes, 52nd Ohio Infantry," pp. 879–82; "Report of Col. Daniel McCook, 52nd Ohio Infantry, Commanding 2nd Brigade, 2nd Division," O. R., Series I, Vol. 30, Part 1, pp. 871–72, 872a; "Report of Maj. General Gordon Granger, U.S. Army, commanding Reserve Corps," O. R., Series I, Vol. 30, Part 1, pp. 852–58; *36th Illinois*, pp. 25–28.

battery, moved from its position at the Gap, and marched out on the left of the army, near McAfee's Church, and took position fronting the enemy. The battery was maneuvered about, taking different positions, in readiness for the expected attack of the enemy. About two in the afternoon the battery was ordered with the brigade, to the support of [Major] General [George H.] Thomas, some distance to the battery's right. They went to Thomas' support on the "double quick." Colonel [Joseph Scott] Fullerton had been ordered back to hurry up the brigade. When it arrived and was taking up position, the battery was ordered into position, and in so doing marched almost into the rebel lines, and to within a hundred yards of one of their batteries. Captain Barnett, with his ever alert presence of mind, as coolly as if he was on dress parade, gave the command, "By the right flank, march," and after marching back a short distance, gave the command, "By the left flank," which brought the battery to the edge of the woods, where a rebel battery opened on Battery I. The battery took position on top of a ridge and went into action, firing a little to the right front, Battery I being about south of the Cloud House, on the west side of the Lafayette road. The rebel batteries were commanded by Captains Swet [Swett] and Fowler; one a six-gun and the other a four-gun, supported by Walther's [Withall's] and Govan's brigades.[4] McCook's brigade moved up to support the battery, and formed immediately in its rear. The woods roared and the earth shook, while shot and shell filled the air with shrieking sounds. The grass and wood in front caught fire, but the battery never moved from its position, but continued the cannonading at the rate of three shots a minute, up to about five o'clock when the gathering gloom of night began to spread its sable wings over the battle field, and about nine at night the battery fired a parting salute, and with McCook's brigade, fell back to Rossville and camped on the old camp ground. It was the last battery to leave the field of Chickamauga.

4. Colonel Daniel C. Govan commanded Liddell's Brigade, and Brigadier General Edward C. Walthall commanded Walthall's Brigade, both of Liddell's Division, of Major General William H. T. Walker's Reserve Corps. The two batteries were Liddell's artillery, commanded by Captain Charles Swett: Fowler's (Alabama) Battery, Captain William H. Fowler and Warren Light (Mississippi Battery), Lieutenant H. Shannon.

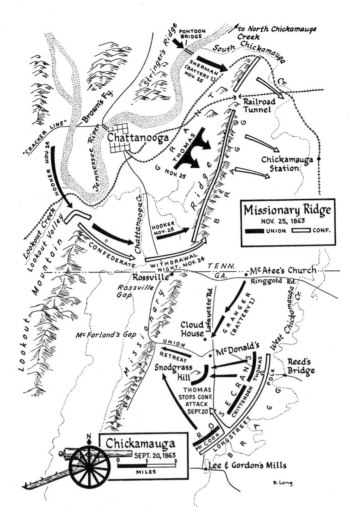

On the morning of the 21st the battery was ordered to the front line on Mission Ridge; one section in the Gap, one on the right, and one on the left. A battalion of the 18th U.S. Regulars was ordered to the support of the left section, but when the rebel skirmish line advanced to within two hundred yards of our lines, the regulars, from some cause, fell back out of the rebel's range leaving the left section unsupported to repulse the attack, but which was bravely done by the cannoneers, giving the rebels double-shotted canister, in such rapid succession, that they were demoralized completely, and fell back out of range of Battery I's guns.[5] As soon as the 125th

5. McCook, in his report said: "The next day my brigade was ordered into position on Mission Ridge. Two guns of Barnett's battery, commanded by Lt. Coe, had a severe affair defending the Ringgold and LaFayette Gaps. He repulsed with cannister three attempts to charge him."—*O. R.*, Series I, Vol. 30, Part 1, p. 871.

Illinois infantry heard that the regulars had fallen back and left the battery unsupported, they came to its support, vowing vengeance on the regulars, if the battery was captured. The left section had two horses wounded in the fight. The Union forces held the Gap till night, when it was abandoned, and the brigade and battery fell back into Chattanooga. General Rosecrans asked Captain Barnett to ride with him into Chattanooga, and while riding along, complimented the Captain and his battery for its work on the 20th and 21st.

The battle of Chickamauga was one of the greatest and most important fought during the war. The Union army had to fall back into Chattanooga, leaving the rebels in possession of the battle field, but they were so badly crippled that they dare not follow up Rosecrans and attack him again, as he still held Chattanooga, his objective point all along. They surrounded him and planted their forces on Missionary Ridge and Lookout Mountain, and cut off his supplies for a short time. All honor to his brave generals and the rank and file, and especially the heroic Thomas, who held his position all through that trying time, and right well was he named the "Rock of Chickamauga."

6. Captain Barnett's report on the battle, which appears in *O. R.*, Series I, Vol. 30, Part 1, pp. 882–83, describes the movements of the battery, as follows:

Battery I, Second Illinois Artillery,
North Chickamauga Creek, Tenn., October 12, 1863.
Sir: I have the honor to make the following report in regard to my participation in the action of September 20 and 21, ultimo:
On the morning of the 20th September, I moved south (with the brigade to which I am attached) from my camp, at the fork of the roads, about three-quarters of a mile south of Rossville, Ga., and after going into position twice, marched 2 miles southwest and found the enemy posted in the woods on the west side of West Chickamauga Creek, near Gaines' Mill. The enemy immediately opened upon us (while we were in column of march, through the burning woods), and we were compelled to move by the right flank into an open field, on the east side of Missionary Ridge, the enemy in the meanwhile shelling us vigorously. Upon the crest of the ridge I went into battery, but the fire in the meantime had extended all over the field, which prevented me from commencing the action until it was extinguished in our front, which duty was performed by the brigade.
At 2 P.M. I opened upon the enemy in my front, and was engaged about one hour, firing very slow, when the enemy brought another battery in position on my right, getting an oblique fire upon me. To these guns I instantly directed my fire, and silenced them in about fifteen minutes. At this time General Turchin came with his brigade from the extreme left of our army, and I assisted him to advance by shelling the enemy from his front, so that he succeeded in gaining shelter, and reformed in the rear of our brigade. I continued firing at intervals until

During the battle the men of Battery I conducted themselves in a praise-worthy manner.[6] Not a man faltered. They proved themselves brave and loyal soldiers, and were worthy of belonging to one of the best batteries that came to the front from the old "Prairie State."

The following description of the battle of Chickamauga is given by Bugler Putney.

Who that was present does not remember the long dusty roads and hazy September days that attended our march towards the great battle field of Chickamauga. To the boys that came from the prairie states, the varied panorama of mountain scenery that for the first time presented itself to their admiring gaze was wonderful and awe-inspiring. Never will it be forgotten, the winding narrow road as it curved around the brow of Lookout Mountain, and the bare walled palisade of its rugged sides. Then the beautiful valley of Chattanooga Creek, with its farms of rich corn, sweet potatoes and pumpkins, all come back to memory, while thinking of the days that preceded that dreadful battle. To me there seemed to be a melancholy sadness pervading the atmosphere, a sort of

---

6 P.M., when I closed the action by two successive six-gun discharges. About 7.30 P.M. we commenced falling back toward Rossville, Ga., which place we reached about 11 P.M., having been engaged four hours, and fired 165 rounds, without any casualties worth mentioning in the battery.

On the 21st, at 12 M., the enemy commenced firing from the heights south of Rossville, and I received orders to move forward from where I was camped a half a mile north of Rossville, on the Chattanooga road. At Rossville I was ordered by General Thomas to place two guns on the hill in the forks of the road, a quarter of a mile above that place. I immediately proceeded with Lieutenant Coe's section, and placed them in the designated position, leaving the remainder of the battery under the hill, in column of pieces faced toward Chattanooga.

About 2 o'clock the enemy opened upon the position with four guns, and continued firing for half an hour, when they ceased, and their infantry came down in line, yelling and shouting, but upon giving them a few rounds of canister (some of them double-shotted) they retreated, nor did they make another charge that day, although their artillery kept up a slow though steady fire until about 5.30 P.M., when we again silenced them after firing 129 rounds. At 8.30 P.M. we withdrew from the hill and arrived at Chattanooga at 11 P.M., no casualties happening upon our side.

My officers and men behaved as usual, doing all that could be done. Lieutenant Coe commanded the section under fire on the 21st.

I remain, very respectfully, your obedient servant,
Chas. M. Barnett,
Captain, Commanding Battery.

Capt. E. L. Anderson,
Acting Assistant Adjutant-General.

impending horror of something terrible to happen, that could not be put aside.

Our camp at Rossville was pitched a few rods north of Rossville Gap. A very few houses gave the name of Rossville to the location, like many other places in the South. The battery lay in camp here from the 14th to the 18th. During the time spent in this camp there was much foraging done for corn, pumpkins and other things that could be used for food. The sweet southern corn was boiled in camp-kettles till tender, then the sweet juicy pumpkins were treated in the same way, both were mixed in equal parts, and then baked in the old fashioned Dutch skillet 'till the crust was rich and brown. Ah, what delicious eating with a soldier's appetite for sauce!

About three o'clock in the afternoon of the 18th orders came for the battery and brigade to move to Reed's Bridge, and burn it to prevent the enemy from crossing Chickamauga Creek. Marching south through the Gap over the Lafayette Road, we moved till we came to a lane leading to the east, which joined the road a little north and opposite McDonald's house. Through this lane, out into the open timber, down into the bottom land of the creek, the brigade marched. Suddenly the battery was halted and ordered to unlimber for action, but the brush was so thick on each side of the road that the battery was obliged to move back to a stony hill, where position was taken for battle. Not being molested the battery camped there for the night, and moved out the next morning after getting breakfast, marching back to the Lafayette road through the same lane. The enemy followed, but the timber hid them from view, yet their skirmishers kept close to the rear guard most of the way; also a battery shelled the woods in our rear. It was during this part of the march that the driver of a rig which consisted of a limber chest on two wheels, packed with medical stores for the vetinary surgeon of the battery, became demoralized by the bursting shells, and lashing his team to a fury, came dashing up the line, entirely oblivious of everything except the idea of escape, charged through the timber alongside of the battery, bounding and swaying from side to side. The boys cheered and jeered, but he noticed it not. The Captain sent an orderly after him post haste, and he was captured and brought back to the battery, where after a severe reprimand he was sent to his place in the line.

General Thomas, at the head of [Brigadier General

John M.] Brannan's Division,[7] marching north, was met at the end of the lane where it joins the Lafayette road, and Colonel Dan McCook told him that the force of rebels this side of the creek was limited in number, probably not more than a brigade, and asked permission to turn back and drive the enemy across the creek, little knowing that the woods this side were full of rebel troops. The enemy following the brigade was [Brigadier] General [Nathan B.] Forrest's cavalry.[8] General Thomas told Colonel McCook to report to his command and he would attend to the enemy in front, so the brigade and battery moved north on the Lafayette road for a short distance, then turned to the right towards the Ringold [Ringgold] road, where the rest of the Reserve Corps was stationed to prevent the enemy from getting around the left flank of Rosecrans' army.

The battery took no part in the battle of the 19th, but lay between the left of Thomas and the forces under General Steedman, at McAfee's Church. Strange to say we did not know that there was any fighting of importance going on about us, and yet the battle on the left of Thomas was only three miles distant, but the next day the roar was very distinct. The night of the 19th the battery camped beside the Ringgold road, not far from the Gap. It was a cold night, and towards morning the men felt more comfortable around the fires than away from them. We were up early, the about eight o'clock moved out a short distance on the Ringgold road, then to the left on a road running north east, which led us to a lowland, where we struck a rebel cavalry camp. The brigade retreated to high ground and went into line of battle; [it] tore a house to pieces and built a fort for the battery, but was ordered about noon to move to the right and take position at McAfee's Church in place of Steedman's division,[9] which had been ordered to the front to reinforce General Thomas, who, by this time, was being badly pushed by Bragg's forces.

At about two o'clock the battery received orders to march

---

7. Brigadier General John M. Brannan commanded the 3rd Division of Thomas's 14th Corps.

8. Brigadier General Nathan B. Forrest commanded a Cavalry Corps of four brigades.

9. Brigadier General James B. Steedman commanded the 1st Division of Granger's Reserve Corps.

to the front, where for the last three or four hours there had been the most infernal roar of battle, that has ever been listened to by man. We marched to our right, across fields and along a country byway. While on the march the battery mail was distributed to the men, and many a boy's heart was made glad by letters from home. Soon evidences of battle began to show in abandoned caisons, scarred trees, and trampled ground where many feet had surged to and fro in furious conflicts. We reached the Lafayette road about opposite the Cloud house, crossed a little run of water, which came from a spring in the Cloud Hill, then moved up a light rise of ground into a small clump of trees and brush, till we came to a point about a hundred rods north of McDonald's house. Here, without warning, we were greeted by two or three shells from a rebel battery, which brought the column to a sudden halt. Orders were soon given to right about face, then again by the left flank through an open field, up a rise, over a ridge, down behind it, and we were out of sight of the rebel battery, but it followed with shells all the time the battery was moving till out of range.

Captain Barnett and Lieutenant Plant rode back to the top of the ridge to see how the land lay and what action should be taken. No sooner did they make their appearance than they were greeted with solid shot which scattered the dirt over them and their horses, causing them to act on the saying, "Discretion is the better part of valor." The rebel shells set fire to the dry sage grass in the open field, which spread towards the crest of the ridge behind which the battery lay, consequently the men had to fight fire for awhile to keep it out of the battery. When all was ready the men unlimbered the guns and ran them up so their muzzles just peeped over the crest, then with a crashing volley Battery I began its part in the battle of Chickamauga. The rebel batteries tried to silence us, but they found they had more on their hands than they had calculated. The position of the battery was well protected by the sharpness of the ridge, while the rebel guns were in an open field northwest of McDonald's house with no

10. Col. Harmon of the 125th Illinois stated: "In approaching the enemy's right their skirmishers appeared and fired upon us, when the brigade moved on double-quick to a strong position on the crest of a high hill, facing the enemy in two lines, I being upon the left and rear. A heavy fire opened on us from two batteries, which was vigorously answered by

cover. They moved from side to side to escape our fire several times, but held their ground till the rebel line fell back east of the Lafayette road at night. About five o'clock a line of rebel infantry formed on the Lafayette road to charge the battery, but double-shotted canister changed their minds, and they fell back out of range. This act on the part of the rebels is only spoken of by the colonel of the 125th Illinois in his report of the part taken in the battle of Chickamauga.[10] Not another officer in the brigade or battery speaks of it. It is strange, for during the impending attack the battery did some of its most rapid firing. A story was afterwards told of one Tom Finnel [Finnell] or "Buffalo Tom," as the boys called him, in connection with this event.

Tom was number two on the gun, that is to take the ammunition from number five and put it into the muzzle of the gun for number one to ram down. There was so much noise and commotion that Tom did not notice that the gun had been fired while he was gone to get more ammunition, [and] returning he was requested to put the load of canister into the gun, by number one, and hurry about it too. Tom refused saying, "There's a load in her already." The sergeant commanded him to put the canister in the gun, which he did, then running off to one side he flattened himself out on the ground and yelled to number four, who pulls the lanyard that fires the gun, "Krist gud, boy, touch her off aizy! Touch her off aizy, or she'll boorst! There's two loads in her! Krist gud, touch her aizy!"

A little later than five o'clock, while a fierce artillery duel was in progress with the two rebel batteries, about two hundred "blue coats" broke through their guns, and for the moment the thought was, the batteries are captured, but soon we noticed that the Union men did not stop running for they came right on through and down the hill towards our battery, finally turning up into our line. The boys stopped firing and commenced cheering, which gave the charging men to understand that they had struck friends, and had found their way out of the threatened circle of enemies. They proved to be a

Barnett's battery. The cannonading continued for an hour and a half; but so hot was Barnett's fire, that he silenced the enemy's guns and their infantry dare not advance."—*O. R.*, Series I, Vol. 30, Part 1, pp. 878–79.

small part of General Turchin's brigade,[11] which had been ordered by General Thomas to clear the way for the retreat of the 14th Army Corps by the Lafayette road to Rossville. General Turchin was with the detachment that came into the battery. His horse having been killed in the charge (one of the 92nd Ohio, who was in the charge declares that one of Battery I's shells did the deed), he had to take it afoot, and when he reached our line he was so badly exhausted that Lieutenant McDonald was obliged to hold him up. Many of the 36th Ohio boys were completely winded when they got inside the battery. One poor boy of that regiment had both legs taken off by a twelve-pound shell about the middle of the battery. He was a brave noble fellow, full of love for his country, and died urging his comrades to give the rebels the best they had left.

About sundown the firing slackened, for the enemy fell back to the east side of the Lafayette road. The battery was practicing at whatever might present, when General Granger, with part of the rim of his hat gone, came from the right, and dismounting, tried his skill in aiming one of the guns. He commanded the Captain to fire a gun every fifteen minutes into the rebel lines, whether he saw anything to fire at or not, which order was carried out to the letter, and a number of rebel campfires must have been made very uncomfortable by shell before the battery retired to Rossville. About nine o'clock, or well after dark, the brigade and battery moved quietly from their position by the left flank, striking the Lafayette road east of the Cloud house, where some of Sheridan's command met us, coming to help us out. Reaching Rossville we went to the old campground and got supper, and stayed the rest of the night. As we moved off the battle field campfires were thick in the rebel lines, and we could hear the low hum of voices in the distance. The same scene presented itself when we reached Rossville where was camped what was left of the Union army.

About half past ten in the forenoon on the 21st we were ordered into the Gap, and one section was sent well out to the

11. Brigadier General John B. Turchin commanded the 3rd Brigade, of Major General Joseph J. Reynolds 4th Division of Thomas's 14th Corps. —See John B. Turchin, *Chickamauga* (Chicago: Fergus Printing Company, 1888), pp. 151–52.

12. Lt. General Daniel H. Hill commanded Hill's Corps; Major General

front on the Lafayette road, with a small support of infantry, for the purpose of retarding a rebel onset, but fortunately a wise order brought them in, long before the charge came, or most of the boys would have been taken prisoners, and the guns would have been captured. In the afternoon all of the guns were placed on the top of the knoll between the Ringgold road and the Lafayette, where they were supported by the Regular brigade, the 19th Illinois, and some other volunteer regiments. About four in the afternoon the rebels advanced in force to determine the Union position and force. They charged, but were stopped before they had gone far by the rapid firing of the batteries on the knoll. At the first rebel yell the Regulars broke and ran down the hill like scared sheep in spite of the efforts of their officers to stop them, nor is it to be wondered at, for they had been terribly cut up the day before, and it was easy to become demoralized after such severe handling. They were soon rallied farther to the rear and brought back to their position. No other effort was made by the rebels that afternoon, and at about eleven o'clock, after winding the wheels of the guns with blankets to deaden the rumble, the battery was let down by prolonges from the hill, and moved off very quietly towards Chattanooga, where it arrived after midnight, and went into camp inside the breast-works.

The enemy in our front, on the battle field, on Sunday afternoon, consisted of two brigades of [Major] General [William H. T.] Walker's division, of [Lieutenant General Daniel H.] Hill's Corps.[12] General Walker, in his report of his part of the battle says, that the Union batteries were served so well that he did not deem it prudent to advance his line under their fire delivered from their position on the Cloud Hill, but he was mistaken in the position, for Battery I was south of the Cloud Hill about forty rods, just across the spring run flowing east.[13]

If any part taken by Battery I during the War of the Rebellion was effectual that done by the battery at the battle of Chickamauga was the most so. Being placed at the extreme

William H. T. Walker's Division, commanded by Brigadier General States R. Gist, was in the Reserve Corps, commanded by Walker.
13. Major General William H. T. Walker's "report" does not say anything about union batteries on Cloud Hill. His report is found in *O. R.*, Series I, Vol. 30, Part 2, pp. 239–44.

left of the army at the latter part of the battle, with the surrounding circumstances such as Steedman having so desperately withstood Longstreet, Thomas having already driven back one effort to outflank the left, the approach of McCook's brigade just as the enemy were about to try to swing around the flank again, the rapid fire of Battery I as if another charge was about to take place, no doubt, made them think they had better re-adjust their lines before trying to attempt again that which they had failed in doing before. In fact General Hill so describes the situation in an article written for the Century Magazine.[14]

Thirty two years have since passed. Again that same field of battle resounds to the tread of many thousand feet. Again does the same sun look down on an armored host marching along its highways with all of the panoply of war. Again does martial music go echoing among the hills and along the valley of the "River of Death" or Chickamauga's stream. What does it mean? 'Tis the nation. 'Tis that same host in part, with those of later years, come to do honor to those whose life blood enriches the battle soil, and to those whose deeds of most heroic bravery the world shall never hear of greater or grander. They have come to dedicate this historical ground as a National Park for the ages and generations to come, where by they may trace the battle lines where once musketry volleyed and cannon thundered, while Death reaped its harvest as the sickle now reaps the grain that is garnered from its field.

Once again does the Bugler of Battery I view the field on the anniversary of the day of battle, but oh, how changed is he and the field. Grayhaired and bent in form he walks where once he rode. The position the battery held is now overgrown with blackberry bushes and thick with small hickory saplings through which a fire has lately passed. The open field in front is planted with corn and sweet potatoes. The woody copse on the Lafayette road has grown and is more dense with undergrowth. That road is a fine graded pike built by the U.S. Government, and extends from Lee & Gordon's Mills on the south to the position held by Sherman's forces at the north end of Missionary Ridge, over twenty miles in length. The land which was occupied by the brigade and battery is

14. Daniel H. Hill, "Chickamauga—The Great Battle of the West," in Vol. 3, pp. 638–62 of *B. & L.* Hill does not say precisely what Putney believes he said.

owned by J. B. Dixon, an Englishman, who married a Southern belle before the war, in the state of Alabama, and since the close of the Rebellion, bought and occupied the farm on the battle field of Chickamauga. Beside the pike, north of where McDonald's house once stood, Mr. Dixon has built a fine residence in front of which is a most elegant lawn tastily laid out, surrounded with a hawthorn hedge and planted with magnolia trees and beautiful flowers. Over this same spot the shot, shell and canister of Battery I once hailed in plentiful fury into rebel ranks. In this same southern home the bugler ate his first meal on the battle field since the day he lunched on hard tack while the battle raged around him.

South of Dixon's house, in the Park, stands four brass cannon pointing in the same direction as did the rebel battery that so bravely withstood the shells of Battery I, and gave as good as was sent. The gun carriages are made of cast iron and stand on granite blocks to prevent the wheels from sinking into the ground and rusting. Silently and peacefully may they remain for years to come ever bearing witness of mispent bravery and fearful waste of life for the unrightous cause of Slavery and a nations sins.

On account of being outside of the Park there is nothing to mark the spot where Battery I stood unless the state of Illinois gets permission of the owner of the land to place a stone marker on the ground. Like Gettysburg, Chickamauga is a field of monuments beautiful and grand in design, attesting the noble lives sacrificed on its blood stained soil.

Rossville is now (1896) a pleasant suburban village of the city of Chattanooga which metropolis has about 40,000 inhabitants, being five times as large as during the war. The old Ross house still stands in a very dilapidated condition, and the spring behind it, runs as cool and pure as when the battery camped there. The knoll that was occupied by the batteries is as steep as ever, but the old trees are gone, and a second growth has taken their place. Two tablets tell what troops occupied the hill, but they do not speak of Battery I nor the Regulars. It is strange how things get mixed in history, but then the origin is mortal. An electric street railway runs from the city to within two miles of the village, and a railroad has a station a short distance west of it. The same road passes through McFarland's Gap and crosses the south end of the battle field, with a station near Snodgrass Hill.

After the battle the battery remained in Chattanooga, an attack being expected, but Bragg determined to starve the "Yanks" out rather than fight, and so settled down to a regular siege.[15] In order to protect the flank of the army on the river, on the 30th of September, McCook's brigade and the battery were sent up opposite the mouth of South Chickamauga Creek, where breastworks were built in a cornfield. The same place was taken afterwards for the north end of the pontoon bridge over which [Major General William T.] Sherman's forces passed to the attack on Missionary Ridge. It was fortunate for the battery that the enemy did not attack here, for they would have had every advantage, as was discovered after crossing the river. From this point the battery moved up to the mouth of North Chickamauga Creek where there is another ford, some six miles above Chattanooga. Here we went into camp, and the sergeants were ordered to build log houses large enough to hold each detachment. The men went to work with a will, and on the second day Sergeant Murphy had his log palace finished and ready to be occupied. Soon all the men were comfortably housed; each house having a large fireplace made of split sticks and plastered with mud, inside and out. A debating society was organized, and many spirited debates were listened to until broken up by the guards ordering "lights out"; and on one occasion the lights not being promptly put out, the men were marched to the guard house.

The rebels occupied the opposite side of the river and watered their horses every day opposite to where the battery horses were

15. Rosecrans had permitted the Union army to be bottled up in Chattanooga, and with Bragg controlling the high ground in front as well as the most direct routes to Stevenson and Bridgeport, the railheads, the army soon was short of food and supplies. Rosecrans did guard the river between Chattanooga and Bridgeport, but the supply line—such as it was —ran from Bridgeport to the northeast, up the Sequatchie River valley to Anderson's, then over the rough Walden's Ridge and down, over the Tennessee River and into Chattanooga. The route was vulnerable to cavalry raids, as General Joseph Weeler's raid of October 1st demonstrated. Until a new supply route could be opened, the Union army was in trouble.

The command and organization of the troops changed after the retreat to Chattanooga. Major General Ulysses S. Grant was placed in charge of all troops between the Alleghanies and the Mississippi River, except for New Orleans. Major General George H. Thomas succeeded to command of the Army of the Cumberland on the 19th of October. His army consisted of:

4th Army Corps, Major General Gordon Granger.

watered, and at such times the "Johnies" and the battery men would have a talk, but as soon as the horses and men had left the river's brink they were ready to shoot at any "Yank" that should show himself.

Foraging parties were sent out every week up to the Sequatchie Valley, and after being gone two or three days, would return loaded with forage for the horses, and beef, hogs, chickens, and whatever could be found in the way of provisions, which proved very acceptable to both men and horses, as the army had been reduced to less than half rations. The men cooped in Chattanooga had a pretty hard time, while the battery boys had more than enough, and their horses were fat and strong. Horses and mules were dying every day in Chattanooga from starvation.

The rebels had possession of Lookout Mountain, and had mounted a battery of heavy guns on the point from which shot and shell could be thrown into the city, making it very uncomfortable for the boys camped in the suburbs. From the camp of Battery I could be seen the flashes of these guns, both night and day, but the damage they did amounted to little compared to the noise they made and the terror they inspired.

October 19th Captain Barnett and Quartermaster Sergeant Brown went to Chattanooga for the purpose of trading the guns of the battery for six three-inch Rodmans. The two Parrotts were turned over to the 7th Indiana Battery, and the James' to a Pennsylvania battery, and the Napoleon guns, to Battery M 1st Ohio

This was the former corps of Crittenden and McCook, consolidated into one. It had

1st Division, Brigadier General Charles Cruft, 2nd Division, Major General Philip H. Sheridan, 3rd Division, Brigadier General Thomas J. Wood

11th Army Corps, Major General Oliver O. Howard

2nd Division, Brigadier General Adolph von Steinwehr, 3rd Division, Major General Carl Schurz

12th Army Corps (Major General Joseph Hooker commanded the 11th and 12th Corps, but personally commanded 1st Division, 4th Corps; 2nd Division, 12th Corps; 12th Division, 15th Corps; and portions of and 14th Corps)

2nd Division: Brigadier General John W. Geary

14th Army Corps, Major General John M. Palmer

1st Division, Brigadier General Richard W. Johnson, 2nd Division, Brigadier General Jefferson C. Davis, 3rd Division, Brigadier Absalom Baird

Artillery. Battery I was now in splendid condition, though every other battery in the Army of the Cumberland was utterly unable to move for want of horses, most of them having died of starvation.[16]

One morning early the whole camp was very much surprised by the rebels opening with a battery from the opposite side of the river on an infantry camp near where the battery had breastworks in the cornfield. They made things lively for a time, and vented some of their spite on the unoccupied works, which showed how warm they could have made it for us had the battery remained in that position.

One of the detailed men was drowned in the mouth of North Chickamauga Creek, while getting forage off an island in the Tennessee River.

On the evening of October 27th the brigade with the battery, was ordered to Brown's Ferry, below Lookout Mountain.[17] The night was dark, and the battery got on to the wrong road, so did not get to the Ferry till about midnight. The next day, about ten o'clock, the battery crossed the river on the pontoon bridge, and took position on a sharp ridge beside the river, it being so steep that the guns had to be pulled up by hand, as the horses could not climb its side. Light breastworks were made and the battery remained here till the 3rd of November. While in this position, to the great surprise of the boys, General Grant mounted on a black horse, carrying a crutch in front of him, came riding up the side of the ridge.[18] His staff followed after

---

Engineer Troops, Brigadier General William F. Smith
Artillery Reserve, Brigadier General John M. Brannan
   1st Division, Col. James Barnett, *2nd Division*
Cavalry
Army of the Tennessee: Major General William T. Sherman, whose immediate command was 11th Corps and 2nd Division, 14th Corps of the Army of the Cumberland, as well as the 2nd and 4th Divisions, 15th Corps and the 2nd Division, 17th Corps.
15th Army Corps: Major General Frank P. Blair, Jr.
   1st Division, Brigadier General Peter J. Osterhous, *2nd Division*, Brigadier General Morgan L. Smith, *4th Division*, Brigadier General Hugh Ewing
17th Army Corps
   2nd Division, Brigadier General John E. Smith
   Battery I was assigned to the artillery of Jefferson C. Davis, 2nd Division of the 14th Corps of the Army of the Cumberland.
16. Not only did almost all the artillery horses die of starvation but the troops were on half rations or less.

on foot, having left their horses at the foot. His object was to examine the rebel breastworks on Lookout Mountain. The General and the officers present did not agree as to their size and number. Grant could not see near as many or as large as the others did, so a large telescope was borrowed from a signal post near by, which fully corroborated Grant's opinion.

The afternoon of the 29th of October forces were seen moving up towards Lookout; for a time, it was not certain whether they were friend or foe, as all thought Bragg would not lose Brown's Ferry without some effort to get it back. Those were intense, eager moments watching that force form its lines. Suddenly "Old Glory" spread its folds to the breeze, then there was a shout went up from the brigade and battery that echoed loud and long among the hills and valleys. Oh, what beautiful, melodious sound those echoes gave on the evening air in those mountain valleys! That same evening the brigade band played a dirge at the funeral of a soldier that had been killed that morning at the Capture of the Ferry. How its solemn tones reverberated and re-echoed along the sides of the mountains, carrying with them a feeling of sweet peaceful sadness, even amidst the tumult of war.

That night Longstreet's forces attacked [Brigadier] General Gerry's [John W. Geary] division,[19] and the roar of battle was kept up till after midnight, while the battery stood ready to take its part

17. The plan was to float some of Brigadier General William B. Hazen's troops down the river to Brown's Ferry; General Turchin marched men from Chattanooga to the Ferry, while Generals Hooker and Palmer brought substantial numbers of troops in from the west and by a circuitous route, from the north. The plan worked perfectly; by 10:00 A.M. on the morning of October 27 a pontoon bridge was across the river and the Tennessee River was open—after a few additional troop movements— from Bridgeport to Lookout Valley. The new supply route made possible by these maneuvers was called the "Cracker Line."

18. Grant had visited Major General Nathaniel P. Banks in New Orleans the preceding August and his horse had shied at a locomotive and fallen on him. His injury was very painful, and for more than a week Grant could not even turn over in bed. On September 25 he was still in bed and needed crutches to walk until the end of November.

19. Brigadier General John W. Geary's Division was unsuccessfully attacked the night of October 28–29, in what has been called the Wauhatchie Night Attack.

should the enemy come its way. In the morning we learned that the Union forces had been victorious, and the beginning of the end of the siege of Chattanooga had taken place.

After the "cracker line" had been thoroughly established, the brigade and battery moved back to the old camp at the mouth of North Chickamauga Creek, where it remained till the battle of Missionary Ridge.

November 12th Captain Barnett received a twenty days' leave of absence and turning the command of the battery over to Lieutenant Plant, left for home. The same day Sergeant Brown proceeded to Nashville, Tenn., to bring up the quartermaster stores of the battery, which had been stored, when the battery left Nashville, August 20th, for the front, and he returned to camp on the 10th of December.

The men of the battery lived a part of the time during the siege on the old fashioned hominy or hulled corn. A large cauldron was found and brought to camp, ashes were leached, and corn hulled in the lye in quantity enough to fill the kettle, then boiled till tender, when all of the bacon drawn for a week's ration for the battery was chopped fine and put into it to grease the corn, all of which was served to the men on large chips or any kind of thing that would hold a ration. The battery had large cribs of corn stored from which all during the siege, the men and horses were fed.

During the stay at North Chickamauga camp the banks of the river were picketed by both rebel and Union soldiers, but owing to an unfortunate shot by one of the brigade boys, killing a rebel patrol, a constant watch was kept by both sides, making it very dangerous to be seen along the shore during the day. Breastworks were built for two guns at the ford, and men stood ready night and day to repel a

20. Sherman's troops were to capture Missionary Ridge by attacking the north end, but the attack of November 24 captured a knob in front of Tunnel Hill, instead of that important defense position. On November 25 Sherman attacked, and after desperate fighting had to be re-inforced, but still was not able to move forward. The simultaneous attacks by Hooker on the left and the so-called "Battle above the clouds" in the center, decided the day and the Confederates, badly beaten, had to withdraw.

21. Brigadier General Jefferson C. Davis, commanding the 2nd Division, reported: "None of my troops participated in the engagement on Mission

rebel crossing. Forage was obtained from an island opposite the mouth of the creek, till the "Johnies" began to resist, which made it too risky to cross over in dugouts.

Pontoon boats and other material having been secretly placed at the mouth of the creek, and disposition of Sherman's forces behind the hills out of sight, having been properly made, at two o'clock in the morning of November 24th, operations began for the battle of Missionary Ridge.[20] A pontoon bridge was thrown across the Tennessee a little below the mouth of South Chickamauga Creek, and about the middle of the afternoon the battery moved across and went into camp a half-mile south of the river, the rest of Sherman's army having reached the north end of the Ridge. On the 25th the battery, now under the command of Lieutenant Plant, moved out of camp in the forenoon, up to the rear of Sherman's forces on the Ridge, near the railroad, and waited there till about three o'clock, when the guns were ordered forward to a position overlooking the western mouth of the tunnel, and soon were engaged in a hot duel with a rebel battery that occupied the crest of the Ridge.[21] The hub of one wheel was struck by a cannon ball and knocked to pieces, while the rim of another was cut, but neither men nor horses were hurt. The duel did not last long, for the attention of the rebel battery was drawn in another direction, so Battery I, not finding anything in particular to fire at, was withdrawn to the rear about sundown, and went into camp in the rear of the forces on the hill. About two o'clock in the morning of the 26th orders came to move out with the division under the command of [Brigadier General] Jeff. C. Davis, and cross South Chickamauga on the pontoon bridge near the mouth. With the orders came the knowledge that Missionary Ridge had been

Ridge except Battery I, Second Illinois Light Artillery. This battery, under command of Lt. Plant, was ordered to the front and took position near the base of the ridge and opened fire on the enemies batteries upon the hill with great spirit. A sharp fire was returned by the enemy's artillery, but owing to the height of the hill upon which his batteries were placed, his fire was very uneffectual, passing too high to do any damage. Supported by General Ewing's division, this battery maintained its position until night."—General Davis "Report," *O. R.*, Series I, Vol. 31, Part 2, p. 491.

taken, and the battery was to join in the pursuit of the rebel army. Soon after crossing the creek the advance struck the rebel pickets and skirmishing continued till our force reached Chickamauga Station where the rebel commissary stores were found in flames, but enough of them were saved to feed the horses of the army for a time. The corn pones and hard-tack our men could not eat outside of rebel prisons. Just east of the Station, on a ridge, the "Johnies" made a stand and commenced shelling our line. Battery I fired a number of rounds,[22] while a force was sent around their flank, and soon they were on the run, leaving their guns. Nothing more was seen of them till just before dark, when their rear guard had a sharp fight with our advance, which continued till into the evening.[23] The battery camped on the south side of a small stream after the skirmish was over, but did not take part in the engagement. The 27th the battery moved to within sight of Ringgold Gap and went into camp with the expectation of staying awhile, but the 28th the line of march was taken towards Knoxville, for the purpose of relieving [Major General Ambrose E.] Burnside who was being besieged by [Lieutenant Ganeral James] Longstreet's forces.[24] The brigade and battery were now permanently attached to the 2nd Division of the 14th Army Corps, commanded by Jeff. C. Davis. On the 29th the brigade camped not far from Cleveland, and December 1st, crossed the Hiawassee [Hiwassee] at Louden [Loudon]. December 5th crossed the Little Tennessee near Morgantown on a trestle bridge, which broke down with the battery, and one of the postillions came

22. "Chickamauga Station was now in full view, presenting a couple of formidable looking field-works, with a large plain intervening, over which we were compelled to move in a direct attack.

"A few shells thrown from a section of Battery I, Second Illinois Light Artillery, failed to bring a reply . . .

"The order to advance and attack the field-works . . . was received with a cheer, and executed with a dash . . . A battery posted in the road opened fire, but was soon driven from its position by Battery I, Second Illinois Light Artillery.

". . . about 3 miles beyond the station . . . a battery opened fire . . . The enemy yielded this position after some sharp skirmishing, and fell back across the open fields where his battery was posted. Battery I, Second Illinois Light Artillery, conforming to the movement of the brigade, moved forward and took position on a commanding hill in the open field, and opened fire upon the enemy's battery."—Brigadier General Jef-

near being drowned in the ice-cold water. He swam and floated down stream for nearly a quarter of a mile before he was rescued by a soldier who rowed out to him in a boat. The division marched about five miles beyond Morgantown, when news having been received that Longstreet had abandoned the siege of Knoxville, the most of Sherman's forces turned back towards Chattanooga.

A very amusing incident occurred on the march back to winter quarters. In some places along the route the road led through dense thickets of young pines. One day the weather being warm, along after midday, the drivers, weary with riding, were lounging in their saddles as they will when the way becomes monotonous. All at once, without an inkling of warning, there burst out of the dense thicket on the side of the road a little black jackass, and with a bray like the roar of a lion he charged the whole length of the battery right beside the teams with tail up and ears back. The drivers dropped out of their saddles as if they had been shot, while the horses tried to run away, but the pines were so thick that they could make but little headway, so were soon caught, and the march was resumed amid much laughter and cheers for the little "black divil," who disappeared as mysteriously as he came. On its return the battery marched through Madisonville and reached Chattanooga, December 15th [18th], and returned to its old camp on North Chickamauga Creek the next day.

This campaign consumed twenty three days of the severest marching the boys of the battery ever experienced. The men were

ferson C. Davis, "Report," *O. R.*, Series I, Vol. 31, Part 2, pp. 491–92.
23. Brigadier General James D. Morgan mentions this action in *O. R.*, Series I, Vol. 31, Part 1, p. 496.
24. Bragg had foolishly sent Longstreet with Major General Lafayette McLaws Division, Hood's Division, Colonel E. P. Alexander's Artillery, Buckner's Division and Wheeler's Cavalry Corps, to attack Major General Ambrose E. Burnside's Army of the Ohio in general area of East Tennessee. As Longstreet's men moved toward him, Burnside collected his forces at Knoxville, Tennessee. The town was under siege conditions from November 17 to December 5, 1863. The climax was an attack on the Union bastion of Ft. Sanders on November 29, which was a failure. Grant sent Sherman with the 4th and 15th Corps to rescue Burnside, but as Sherman's troops approached Knoxville, Longstreet ended the siege and moved away. Sherman left Granger with two divisions at Knoxville and ordered the rest of his troops back to Chattanooga.

poorly clothed and fed; subsisting on "flapjacks" and molasses, and only half enough of them. The army lived off of the country mostly, and the infantry had no tents of any kind. The boys did not suffer in that line, as they had their tarpaulins to shelter them against storms. The weather was very cold and caused suffering from lack of clothes and shelter, but the soldiers bore up without much complaint, except occasionally they would say, half in earnest and half in jest, "Oh, my country, my bleeding country! How I suffer for thee!" Most every infantryman had holes burnt in his scant clothing from sleeping too near the fire built of cedar rails, which had a spiteful way of throwing coals of fire on a man's head or bed and did not care a snap about it either.

December 24th Captain Barnett rejoined the battery from leave of absence, and the boys were glad to see him once more in command. Sergeant McDonald also received his commission as Junior 2nd Lieutenant, to date from March [1], 1863, but was not mustered in as Lieutenant until March [1], 1864.[25]

25. Captain Barnett recommended on December 16, 1863, 1st Sergeant Charles McDonald, for Junior 2nd Lieutenant, *vice* Lt. Haight. He pointed out McDonald's "good behavior, capacity and courage in action." The Illinois Adjutant General noted on the back of Barnett's letter "Commission issued Dec. 16, 1863."

26. Enlistments in the Union army had been for varying lengths of time, particularly in the early days of the war. Over all, it had been possible to enlist for three months, for one hundred days, for one or for two or for three years. The government favored an enlistment that would be for "three years or during the war," presumably whichever was shorter. An army composed principally of volunteers serving for varying lengths of time, in which the volunteers often went home at the expiration of their service, is not a very stable organization. In 1864, for example, the soldiers who enlisted for three years in 1861 would be leaving for home all through the late spring, summer, and fall.

Then too, as the war progressed, the armies required more and more men, and preparations were made for a draft. Will County, Illinois, from where many of the Battery I men came, enrolled or listed all men of military age in the month of October, 1862. President Lincoln, in his call for 300,000 volunteers on October 19, 1863, authorized a draft to begin January 5, 1864, in any state which did not meet its quota.

In an effort to stabilize the army by extending the period of service of volunteers and to ease the recruiting situation, the Adjutant General's office in the War Department on June 25, 1863 issued General Orders 191, authorizing veteran volunteers. "In order to increase armies now in the field" is the way the order began; it generally authorized a force of "veteran volunteers" to be enlisted for three years or during the war, of

On Christmas the sergeants held a meeting in the quarter-master's quarters—the object of which was to discuss the subject of "enlistment for the war." [26] The order from the war department was read, and was in substance as follows: all enlisted men who had served two years since the war began, could be re-enlisted for three years or to the close of the war. They would be mustered out and mustered in, and receive a bounty of $400, to be paid in installments, but were to receive $200 down, as soon as papers were signed; also they were to receive all back pay and a furlough for thirty days. After the sergeants had favorably talked it all over, Quartermaster Sergeant Brown was called on for his views. He said that, in his opinion, the next campaign would be the last the battery would have to serve, that the men of the battery who re-enlisted would not be in the service over one year longer than their original time of three year's enlistment, all of which proved to be true, for the men were all mustered out before serving nine months over their first enlistment. Sergeant Murphy declared that he had enlisted for "during the war,"

men between 18 and 45, previously enlisted who had served not less than nine months. Veteran volunteers would receive a month's pay in advance and a bounty and premium of $402.00 and a thirty-day furlough. The money was to be paid:

1. Upon being mustered into service as a veteran volunteer:

one month's pay in advance	$13.00
First installment of bounty	25.00
Premium	2.00
	40.00

2. First regular pay day (or 2 months after muster in) 50.00
3. First regular pay day after 6 months service 50.00
4. First regular pay day after 1 year of service 50.00
5. First regular pay day after 18 months of service 50.00
6. First regular pay day after 2 years of service 50.00
7. First regular pay day after 2½ years of service 50.00
8. At expiration of 3 years service 75.00

The plan was modified, interpreted and extended in General Orders 216, 305, 324, 345, 359, 376 and 387 for 1863, but the basic idea remained: to re-enlist troops in the field for three years or the length of the war.

Battery I would end its original term of service on December 31, 1864; a number of its men (either 64 or 65, it is impossible to be certain) did re-enlist as veteran volunteers. The one effect, perhaps not anticipated in Washington, was pointed out by Major General George H. Thomas in his "Report" of operations for January and February, 1864: "The army at this period had been very much weakened by the absence of many regiments, who had gone to their respective states to reorganize as veteran volunteers . . . so that in making my preparations I found but a small force available."—O. R., Series I, Vol. 32, Part 1, p. 8.

and should it last seventeen years, and he was alive, he would still be in it. He thought that the government had a very fair offer to the boys, that they should take the thirty days' furlough, come back to the front and remain there till "this cruel war was over." The other sergeants made remarks of similar nature, and much enthusiasm was shown in favor of re-enlistment.

December 26th the battery broke camp and marched to a point six miles southeast of Chattanooga, and camped near McAfee's Church, on the extreme left of Chickamauga battlefield. It rained all day and camp was not reached till most night, everything was wet through and through, taps had sounded, and most of the men had gone to their "pup-tents" for the night, when the bugle sounded the assembly, and the men had to crawl out in the rain and get into line; the orderly sergeant came out of the Captain's tent with a candle covered with a hat to keep the rain off while he read general orders for re-enlistment. One can imagine how anything of that nature would seem to soldiers on such a night, but when the warm sunshine came and the men began to look over the matter, every man that could enlist gave his name to his country for three years or "during the war."

December 31st the battery marched back to Chattanooga, and crossed the river to the north side, and went into camp beside a ravine, a short distance from the river, in the slush and mud. New Year's Eve the men laid down in muddy beds to wake towards midnight to find their blankets and boots frozen into the ground. No more sleep that night, but large fires were built and the boys stood around them, thawing on one side and freezing on the other. The next morning the battery moved across to the south side again, by the swing ferry, as the ice in the river had broken the pontoon bridge. The battery was parked beside a brick church, and all of the stores were put inside to remain till the battery returned from their furlough.

January 2nd, 1864, sixty four [27] old members of Battery I were

27. Woodruff says 65 decided to re-enlist.—*Woodruff*, p. 430.
28. The *Report* of the Illinois Adjutant General says the men received their furloughs on January 16. The (Springfield) *Illinois State Journal*

"mustered out" and then "mustered in" again to the service "for the war"; next day paid off, and were ready for Uncle Sam to take them to their northern homes for a "happy-go-lucky" time. Oh, what a jolly set there was that night in the old brick church, during that long cold wait for morning! How many imitative cats, dogs, mules, jackasses, roosters, hens, &c., made night hideous, while the officers plead for order and silence. The next forenoon part of the men started for Bridgeport with the horses, while the rest waited for passage down the river on the steamboat which did not start till after dark, and did not get to Bridgeport till midnight.

January 4th the men started for Springfield, Ills., where they arrived after having spent two nights in Nashville, and one in Louisville, and one on the cars in Indiana. Upon alighting from the cars the boys were given their furloughs for thirty days by Captain Barnett, who with Sergeant Brown, had preceded the men by one day, so as to have their papers ready and there should be no delay, and the men could take the first train for their homes. Each man on receiving his furlough was ordered to report to Captain Barnett, at Joliet, Ills., at the expiration of thirty days.[28] What good-byes and good wishes for the best kind of a time were given by the boys as they separated.

The men had been away from their homes for two long eventful years as none but the officers had received leaves of absence, and now they were to enjoy a well earned furlough. What thrilling stories of long marches and hard fought battles they had to rehearse, when they were seated around the home firesides amongst the old familiar scenes of their boyhood. All too soon would their furloughs end, and then the long bloody campaigns were before them when the spring should come again. "Eat, drink, and be merry, for tomorrow ye may die" was plainly evident from past experience, and they were ready when the time came to go to the front, bravely battling under the folds of "Old Glory" for their country, one and inseparable. All felt that the next season of war would end the Rebellion, and that there

on March 19 said, "Battery I, 2nd Artillery . . . are to be mustered and paid off at Camp Yates today." These, of course, were the Battery I men who did not choose to re-enlist.

would be desperate fighting. They were willing to stay at the front till the "last armed foe" expired, and they could lay aside the implements of war and take up once more, in peace, the tools they had thrown down when the first shot at Fort Sumter rang the knell of fearful war, and caused President Lincoln to call them to the defense of their country and the glorious stars and stripes.

During the stay north the battery was recruited up to its full membership. The roster, at that time, of commissioned and non-commissioned officers was as follows: Charles M. Barnett, Captain; H. B. Plant, Sr. 1st Lieutenant; Alonzo W. Coe, Jr. 1st Lieutenant; Judson Rich, Sr. 2nd Lieutenant; Charles McDonald, Jr. 2nd Lieutenant; Orderly Sergeant, George T. Ward; Quartermaster Sergeant, T. C. S. Brown; Sergeants: Z. Miller; Hiram Hill; S. J. Murphy; Robert Heath. The battery was now where it first organized, after two years of service in marching and fighting at the front, having lost nearly one third of its members from disease and wounds and killed, and those that were discharged for disability. The recruits of the battery, who had not been in service long enough to re-enlist, were left in camp Chattanooga, Tenn., in command of Ed. Smith, who had recently enlisted in the battery.

The camp of Rendezvous at Joliet, Ill., was located near the cemetery, on the east side of the city.[29] Barracks had been erected for the accomodation of troops, which were very comfortable, after having served in "pup tents" for shelter. The 66th Illinois Reg't rendezvoused at the same time with the battery, and all remember the jolly hours spent there while waiting for orders to return to the front. There was one pleasant incident occurred, which will be long held in memory by all who took part. A number of the boys in the battery had their homes in Aurora, Ill., and their young lady friends, to show their appreciation of the boys who wore the "blue," and the cause they were so willingly and bravely battling for, presented the battery with a guidon to carry through the rest of its campaigns, to which presentation a suitable and eloquent reply was made by one of the members of the battery. It is needless to say that that guidon was proudly and safely carried through the campaigns of Atlanta,

29. This camp at Joliet was called Camp Erwin. — *Woodruff*, p. 430.

Savannah, South and North Carolinas, and returned at the end of the war to Aurora, where now it reposes as one of the cherished relics of the war that adorn the walls of the beautiful hall of the Aurora Post of the G.A.R.

On MARCH 4th, after a two weeks' extension of furlough,[1] the battery "veterans" boarded the cars of the Michigan Central R. R. to procede to the front, viz. Indianapolis, Ind., Louisville, Ky., and Nashville, Tenn., to Chattanooga, Tenn., at which place they arrived March 8th, and joined the men left in charge of the guns and camp equipage. Ed. Smith, in command of camp, had everything in good shape. Lieutenant Coe, with a detail of men, was left in Nashville to procure horses for the battery, as there had to be a new supply in place of those turned over when the battery went home on

1. The Battery reported to Camp Erwin at Joliet on February 15 and then was granted an additional two weeks leave.
2. On January 25, 1864, 1st Lt. Coe wrote to General Fuller, recommending Judson Rich, a Senior 2nd Lt. be promoted to Junior 1st Lt., *vice*

5

THE

ATLANTA CAMPAIGN

*In which Battery I rendezvous at Joliet as its veteran re-enlistment fur-
loughs end, then moves to Chattanooga, Tennessee, arriving March 8,
1864, to prepare for the Atlanta campaign. On May 7, the Battery went
into action, and was constantly either in action or on the move. It did some
spectacular shooting near Kenesaw Mountain, recorded by a Chicago
Tribune correspondent. As Sherman reached out to the right of Atlanta
the Battery suffered its worst casualties of the war. Meanwhile, General
John B. Hood replaced Johnston as commander on July 17, and after his
attacks on Sherman failed to halt the Union advance, Hood retreated from
Atlanta to Lovejoy's Station. Soon Hood headed north, and Battery I was
among the troops sent north to head him off; Sherman followed Hood but
shortly gave up the pursuit and, after reinforcing Thomas around Nashville, prepared to march from Atlanta to the sea.*

furlough. He was successful in getting a fine lot of very good horses,
and soon joined the battery in Wauhatchie Valley whither the
battery had moved from Chattanooga. The first few days after the
return was occupied in getting things into shape and drilling the
new recruits.

March 23rd Lieutenant McDonald was mustered into service as
Jr. 2nd Lieutenant, and Sergeant George T. Ward was promoted to
Orderly Sergeant.[2]

March 21st the battery was ordered to report to the commander

Lt. Plant, and 1st Sgt. George T. Ward be promoted to Junior 2nd Lt.,
vice Lt. McDonald, soon to be Senior 2nd Lt. Coe pointed out he had only
one officer with him, Barnett being absent as Chief of Artillery, 2nd Division, 14th Army Corps and McDonald had been captured.

of the Twentieth Corps for duty, and moved out to Lookout Valley, six miles from Chattanooga. That night there was a heavy fall of snow, nearly a foot in depth, for which the men were poorly provided, having but few tents up. On the 26th Lieutenant Rich arrived from Springfield, Ill., with some new recruits. Soon after he was taken with smallpox and had to be treated outside of the battery in a small hut built expressly for him and his nurse. He recovered in good shape, and there were no other cases in the battery. During some of the first days of April the battery practiced target shooting, which was witnessed by experienced artillery officers, and they gave the boys credit for doing as good shooting as they had ever seen done.

While the battery was with the Twentieth Corps [3] the officers of the 2nd Division signed a petition, requesting that Battery I, Captain Barnett commanding, be assigned to the 2nd Division of the 14th Army Corps, to which it had belonged before the veterans had received their furlough; and the petitioners forwarded the same to General Thomas. The result was that April 9th orders were received by Captain Barnett, assigning his command to the 2nd Division, commanded by Jeff. C. Davis, and moved the same day to Rossville Gap, where the division was encamped. The boys were very glad to get back to the old command where they could march and fight beside their old trusted and tried brigade commanded by Colonel Dan. McCook.[4] How the old brigade cheered when Battery I moved into camp, and how the boys yelled and swung their hats in reply. All felt the greatest satisfaction that the battery had gotten back to its old place among old comrades to remain during the rest of the war.

Captain Barnett was appointed Chief of Artillery of the 2nd Division by General Davis; Captain Barnett then relieved Quartermaster Sergeant Brown as quartermaster for the battery, and made him his clerk, and called upon Thomas Betts to act as quartermaster,

3. There is no record of Battery I being transferred to the 20th Corps. It was transferred to the artillery of the 1st Division, 11th Army Corps, on March 18, but on April 8 came back to the artillery of Brigadier General Jefferson C. Davis' 2nd Division of Major General John M. Palmer's 14th Army Corps, Army of the Cumberland. Throughout the month of April,

which position Betts retained until the battery was mustered out of service. During the stay in this camp the battery did considerable target practice.

One day the Captain thought he would test the accuracy of the practice, so men were sent out to watch the effect of the shells and caseshot who were to keep tally of every time the target was hit, and whether a miss was made to the left or right, above or below. The bugler and another man were the ones chosen for the markers. They repaired to their station and the first gun was fired, but instead of hitting the target the shell exploded to the right and in just the position to send the pieces whistling around the ears of the markers. Of course there had to be a change of base on their part. The next gun fired, the next, and next, in rapid succession, with like defective explosions and like dodging of flying pieces. All marks of results, so far, were unintelligible hieroglyphics. The bugler left his companion to take notes while he reported the condition of circumstances. The Captain suggested that the parties might climb a tree far enough away to be safe, and there mark the result of the practice, which advice was acted upon by climbing the highest tree that could be found in the vicinity. The right gun fired a caseshot which exploded about thirty yards from the muzzle, and the pieces seemed to be looking "for a lodge in some vast wilderness" or two fellows lodged in a treetop. The twigs and leaves fell around them while they immediately got out of that tree, thinking that they could descend better by a conscious understanding than an unconscious gravitation and with a better chance to escape the wrath to come, after reaching terra firma. The demoralized markers made their way to the Captain and reported the result of their observations with the request that they be allowed the privilege, if not compatible with the good of the service, of dying or being killed at the front by the hand of an enemy rather than by the hands of their friends while in pursuit of knowledge. The Captain granted their request and cursed

forty enlisted men from the 2nd Independent Battery, Minnesota Light Artillery, served with Battery I.

4. Colonel Daniel McCook commanded the 3rd Brigade in the 2nd Division of the 14th Army Corps. Brigade troops were these: 85th, 86th, 110th and 125th Illinois Infantry, 22nd Indiana Infantry and 52nd Ohio Infantry.

Atlanta Campaign
1864

MILES

the ammunition. A few days after the Captain reported the condition of the ammunition to the general commanding, and was told to use it up as fast as he could in his drills so as to get rid of it, and then get a supply of new in its place. Soon after the battery went out to drill and commenced firing with so much fury that the general thought the camp was being attacked and came rushing out to see what was the matter, but finding that Battery I was the cause of all the commotion, ordered the rest of the ammunition to be buried rather than have so much noise and confusion.

On the 2nd of May, 1864, the division was ordered to Ringgold, Ga., and went into camp till the 5th, when it marched to Catoosa Springs.[5] Early in the morning of the 7th the division moved to Tunnel Hill, arriving there at eleven in the forenoon, and going immediately into action in a duel with a rebel battery, driving it away from its position.[6] A line of skirmishers in front of the rebel line of battle seemed to hold their position regardless of infantry or artillery fire. The battery expended quite a number of round of shell, trying to demoralize them, but when the rebel line fell back to Buzzard [Buzzard's] Roost [Gap] the skirmishers were found to be dummies stuffed with straw. Captain Barnett received a close call when the advance was made to Tunnel Hill after the rebels had evacuated that position, as he was riding with the staff of the corps commander for the purpose of locating batteries on the crest of the Hill. The general had just reached the brow of the hill when a detachment left as rear guard, rose from an ambush and fired point blank into the staff, wounding some two or three but killing none. The rebels then turned and fled.

The 8th was an idle day for the battery, but they had the pleasure of witnessing some very fine skirmishing done by the brigade, across the valley, between Tunnel Hill and Rocky Face Ridge. Buzzard's Roost Gap is a pass through Rocky Face, which is a ridge with a precipitous face of about fifty or a hundred feet of limestone, which it

5. Battery I was about to participate in the campaign for Atlanta. Basically this was a campaign of maneuver in which Sherman avoided frontal attacks—except for the failure at Kenesaw Mountain—and instead outflanked the Confederates led by General Joseph E. Johnston. Johnston was given the Confederate command after Bragg lost Chattanooga. He led the Army of Tennessee (Hardee and Hood commanding the two corps) and General Leonidas Polk's Army of Mississippi. Grant was now in charge of all union armies and was in the east; Sherman's forces were the Army of the Cumberland (Thomas), the Army of the Tennessee (Major General James B. McPherson) and the Army of the Ohio (Major General John M. Schofield). The war of maneuver would end when Johnston was succeeded by General John B. Hood; Hood's attacks near the end of the campaign were unsuccessful and hastened the fall of of Atlanta.

6. Captain Charles M. Barnett's Report of the Atlanta Campaign says the Battery fired "60 rounds at a rebel battery, which retired." *O. R.*, Series I, Vol. 38, Part 1, pp. 829–30. (This report cited hereafter as *Barnett.*) Battery I had the dubious honor of firing the first gun in the 14th Corps in the Atlanta campaign.

is impossible to climb. The skirmishers reached this far and could get no farther. Late in the afternoon of the 9th the battery was moved to a position not far from the Gap, and worked all night building works for the guns,[7] and the next morning opened fire on whatever presented, especially the rebel sharpshooters. One plucky fellow on the ridge, bothered the boys very much from his position behind an enormous boulder. It was determined to dislodge him, so the battery opened on the rock with percussion shell, and soon the pieces of rock and gravel began to fly about his ears to such a degree that he became demoralized and started to run, when another battery seeing the fun, opened on him also. Shells exploded all around him, now he is up and now he is down, yet he still is able to flee and seems to bear a charmed life. He gains the top of the ridge and gets out of sight in spite of every effort to kill him. At night the battery moved back to Tunnel Hill and camped in a plowed field and the horses were unharnessed for the first time in thirty six hours.[8] About midnight a violent thunder storm struck the camp, blowing down tents and drenching the boys so they had to spend the rest of the night drying their clothes before rousing fires, while the air rang with yells and hootings on both sides of the lines. Early on the morning of the 11th the battery went into action in a gap near the railroad and fired forty rounds.

At six in the morning of the 12th the bugle sounded "drivers mount," and the division marched towards Snake Creek Gap, reaching it about dark. The road was rough and crooked for a night's march, but the hour of midnight saw the battery in camp at the south end, and about noon on the 13th the division moved towards the line of battle around Resaca. An amusing incident occurred while moving to the front. The troops were marching east from the mouth of Snake Creek Gap by a narrow country road, when the brigade and battery halted for another division to move into the battle ahead. Beside the road was a log shanty, newly built, and on

---

7. "Captain Barnett, my Chief of Artillery, with much difficulty succeeded in getting a part of his artillery in position, and operated very successfully with it against the enemy's batteries and works."—Major General Jefferson C. Davis, "Report," *O. R.*, Series I, Vol. 38, Part 1, p. 627.

8. The battery fired "196 rounds at the enemy; at night fell back, and

a rudely constructed bench outside the door sat a very good looking young woman of the southern "cracker" type. She had been watching the soldiers file past on the road, and seemed to sit there in a listless mood, regardless of the gaze of the men as they stood looking at her. Finally the boys began to guy her with questions in somewhat after this manner: "Are you married?" "Yaas." "Where is your husband?" "Oh, he's down yander." "You'ens gwine down whar he is." "Ar'n't you afraid we'll kill him?" "Dunno. Maybe he'll kill you'ens. "How many Rebs are there down yonder?" "Dunno, a heep on'em. We'ens got a right smart crowd." "What will you do if the Yanks kill your husband?" "Dunno"; and then a smile seemed to creep over her face, which deepened into a grin, then hitching along on the bench she said: "Dunno, I 'spect I'd hab to marry one ob you'ens." There was a burst of laughter from all the listening crowd, and just then the bugles sounded forward, and the column moved on toward the battle smoke and roar.

The battery took position on a hill with a small stream in front, on the east side of which was the rebel breastworks. A light line of works was thrown up in front of the guns heavy enough to protect from musketry. The 15th was spent in firing on the line in front, and shelling the woods to the right and left. The "Johnies" tried to silence the guns by keeping up a constant fire of musketry, but their aim was high so most of the harm done was in the rear where the battery wagons and horses were kept to be out of the way of danger. One horse was killed, and a man wounded in the battery. At night the battery fired a shot every fifteen minutes, and there was a charge made by the rebels, which was handsomely repulsed by the battery.

During the time the battery occupied the hill,[9] water for the men to drink was brought from the rear by men detailed for that purpose. One of the number was a short, stout, little Frenchman, who had enlisted at Joliet while he was gloriously drunk, and had sobered up

took the harness off for the first time in thirty-six hours."—*Barnett*, p. 829.

9. On the morning of the 16th, one section of the battery was detailed with the 125th Illinois to guard the division supply and ordinance train.— See Captain George W. Cook's "Report," *O. R.*, Series I, Vol. 38, Part 1, pp. 723–24.

to find himself a soldier in Uncle Sam's service. He could throw more dirt in digging breastworks than any other three men in the battery, if he thought that there was to be an attack on the lines. He did not like to be at the front, if he could help it, so he was given work at the rear when possible. The boys knew his nature, so when they saw him skirmishing from tree to tree with a pail of water, they began to throw small stones at him, which he thought were bullets. As soon as he left the cover of a tree the stones would strike thick around him, and he, in his fear, took them to be rebel lead. With one hand on the ground and the pail in the other he would aim for the next tree, head down. Finally he failed to reckon the distance correctly, and, head on, struck the tree doubling himself up and spilling every drop of water in his pail. There was a roar of laughter from the boys, which the Frenchman heard, and now comprehending the whole plot, got up and swinging his fists, swore in all the strength of his French and English vocabulary, then, with body bent, started back for more water.

On account of the movements made by the Army of the Tennessee on the right the enemy were obliged to evacuate their works at Resaca on the night of the 16th, and fall back to a line of works south of the Oostenaula River, near Adairsville. In the morning the boys went over the ground which had been fought over, and found the top of the skull which had been blown off by one of Battery I's shells, while flesh and brains were scattered all around in the works.

General Jeff. C. Davis' 2nd Division of the 14th Army Corps, was ordered to take the road to Rome, Ga., and in the afternoon, about two o'clock, struck the enemy two miles from that city, north. The battery immediately began shelling a piece of woods, while the brigade advanced to flank them. A sharp fight took place in which the brigade lost some eighty men killed and wounded. The Rebs retreated and the division pursued till within sight of the city, when a rebel battery south of the Coosa River opened on Battery I with

10. "A battery of the enemy's stationed on the opposite side of the Coosa River, having opened fire on my line, Captain Barnett's battery reported to me and was soon in a good position, and in a short time silenced that of

heavy guns, but did not keep up the duel very long as their retreat was continued that night [18th]. On the 18th the battery remained on the north side of the Oostenaula, and May 19th a pontoon bridge having been thrown across the river, the division crossed over and took possession of the city and the rebel works. On the 21st the battery crossed and went into camp inside the city limits.

The editor and compositors of the "Rome Courier," a weekly paper, having left with the rebel troops, some Yankee types of the division took possession of the office with the intention of publishing the other half of the paper, left unprinted; but the boys were so anxious to get Rebel news that their copy was all taken before the Yanks were ready to work, so an issue was made in its stead, of the "Tri Weekly Union," of which Comrade S. J. Murphy has a copy, and which he cherishes as a souvenir of the occupation of Rome, Ga., by the Union army.

The citizens of Rome were very much frightened, they having heard so much of Yankee barbarity, formed the idea that the invading forces under Sherman would show no mercy after the capture of their beloved city. The mills and foundries used by the Confederacy were destroyed. There were a number of forts armed with heavy guns, which were taken and made use of in fortifying the city by the Union forces.

It was thought that the 2nd Division would do garrison duty here, so General Davis, with his staff, began looking about for a good point to place a battery that should overlook the whole city and country around. Riding to the highest point, there was found a very fine house and beautiful front yard full of flowers and shrubs. Opening the gate the general and staff rode in, and were not careful to keep off of the flower beds or nice graveled walks with their horses. The front door opened and out came an old lady very much enraged, calling at the top of her voice for the party to get out of her yard or she would have every one of them arrested forthwith. The general told her to get ready to move her things out of the house

the enemy."—Brigadier General James D. Morgan, "Report," *O. R.*, Series I, Vol. 38, Part 1, p. 647.

immediately as he intended to plant a battery there right away. In a shrill, cracked voice the old lady exclaimed: "No, you won't plant a battery in this yard. There is enough planted in this yard already. I won't have anything more in this lot, so you get right out of here, or you'll wish you had." The general explained matters to her as well as he could, and advised her to move out quietly thus saving her household furniture. She did not fully realize the condition of things till she saw the fine brick house being torn down over her head, then she went about weeping and wringing her hands while the boys took pity on her and helped put her effects to one side so no harm should come to them. The next day a heavy fort stood where once had been a beautiful Southern home.

Alas for hopes of garrison duty! On May 24th [23rd] the division took up the line of march from Rome, crossing the Etowah River near its mouth, marching twenty-five miles that day, and going into camp in a violent rainstorm. On the 25th the battery made a forced march over very bad roads, not making much headway, and late in the evening cannonading was heard in the direction of Dallas. On the 26th the battery arrived at Dallas, with the division, at five in the afternoon, and went into position on Sherman Hill. The battery stayed in this position till June 1st, when it fell back at night and fed the horses without unharnessing them, the drivers lying down by their teams and the cannoneers by the guns. The sergeants were sent to the front with instructions to remain during the night, and if the enemy attacked to return to the battery immediately and give alarm. The rebels had made several charges on the Union line where the battery had been in position for the past few days, but with disastrous results to the "Johnies." The command remained in this position at Dallas from the 26th of May till the 1st of June, being compelled to "lie on its arms," not knowing what moment it would be attacked.

Sherman's army had made a detour to the right of the railroad in order to turn the strong position at Altoona [Allatoona] Pass, which the enemy had determined to hold at all hazards. Dallas was the point of concentration, but [Major General Joseph] Hooker struck the enemy moving in the same direction at New Hope Church, and a severe fight took place, which caused the 14th and 20th Corps to stop there while [Major General James B.] McPherson's Corps, with Jeff. C. Davis' division was fighting at Dallas. The distance between the two places is four miles, New Hope being a little north east of Dallas.

On the 1st of June [11] the battery started for New Hope towards evening with the guns alone, leaving the caisons in charge of Bugler Putney, which were to move later. Starting out about sundown on an indistinct trail across the country he, without a guide, led the way till he reached a point where there was a well traveled road running east, and a light trail led to the northeast beside a steep hill. He was puzzled which to take, but finally decided to go east on the well traveled road. Followed by the caisons he had gone about forty rods, when the word "halt" was heard, and almost immediately a bullet whizzed past. The column halted, was turned back, with as little noise as possible, expecting every minute to be "gobbled up" by the "Johnies." The other trail was taken, but had not gone far before one of the caisons, which had gotten out of the path on account of the darkness which made it very hard to pick the way, turned a complete somerset, horses as well, landing all right on its wheels against a tree. Putney decided to stay where they were until some one came to guide them out of a very puzzling condition. A little after daylight a sergeant came back from the guns to look up the caisons, battery wagons, and spare horses. The camp of the caisons could not have been more than a quarter of a mile from the rebel line with no support of any kind. The battery laid in reserve from the 2nd of June till the 5th behind the position at New Hope Church, and on June 6th [5th] it marched to near Ackworth [Acworth], Ga., and camped not far from the railroad.

June 7th Lieutenant McDonald and Warren Dibirt were ordered by the Captain to go outside of the lines to look for forage. They had gone but a short distance when they were captured and held as prisoners of war until the collapse of the Confederacy. They

11. Throughout the month of June, 38 enlisted men from the 2nd Independent Battery, Minnesota Light Artillery, were detached to serve with Battery I.

rejoined the battery at Washington, D.C., and were hardly recognized by their old comrades on account of their pitiable condition.

Heavy thunder showers were of daily occurrence accompanied by vivid lightning. The roads soon became quagmires, if traveled much, and the men were drenched most of the time.

On the morning of the 10th the division moved forward in the direction of Big Shanty. To the left and on the east side of the railroad were Sweet Mountain and Black Jack; to the west, and nearly in front, was Kenesaw Mountain, and to the right were Lost and Pine Mountains. Here the enemy was found strongly fortified. General Sherman says in his official report: "The scene was enchanting; too beautiful to be disturbed by the harsh clamor of war; but the Chattahoochee lay beyond, and I had to reach it." [12]

On the 11th, the railroad being repaired up to the very skirmish line, a loaded train of cars came to Big Shanty. The locomotive detached, was run forward to a water tank within the range of the enemy's guns on Kenesaw, whence the Rebs opened fire on the locomotive; but the engineer was not afraid, went on to the tank, got water, and returned again safely to his train, answering the guns with the screams of his engine whistle, while the whole army cheered with shout upon shout. [13]

On the 14th the battery was facing Pine Mountain on which the rebels were building breastworks in plain view. General Sherman and his staff rode along the line, and noticing the presence of the "Johnies" in a squad on the mountain, ordered Battery I and an Indiana battery to open on them. After a few shots quite a sensation was observed as if some important officer had been hurt or killed. A day or two afterwards it was known that the rebel [Lieutenant] General [Leonidas] Polk, was dead from a shell striking him in the

12. *O. R.*, Series I, Vol. 38, Part 1, p. 67.
13. This paragraph is a thinly disguised version of a paragraph in Sherman's *Memoirs.*—See *Memoirs of General William T. Sherman by Himself. Foreword by B. H. Liddell Hart*, 2 vols. (Bloomington, Indiana: Indiana University Press, 1957), Vol. 2, p. 51. All references will be to this edition, which will be cited hereafter as *Sherman.*
14. Lt. General Leonidas Polk was indeed killed on Pine Mountain on June 14, by a shell from a Parrott gun. Sherman says he ordered General Howard to fire on the group of Confederates in plain sight on Pine Mountain. *Barnett* does not mention this incident.—See *Sherman*, Vol. 2, pp. 53–54.

breast at the time the batteries were shelling the mountain.[14] The Indiana battery claimed the glory of killing him, and it may have done the deed.

The men worked all night the 14th building bastions for the guns into which they moved in the morning of the 15th, and shelled the rebel works all day. The general lines were advanced, so there was much skirmishing which made the day one of great excitement, as all anticipated a general engagement at any moment. Pine Mountain was abandoned, and an incessant roar of artillery on the right, showed that Sherman's "flanking machine" was in motion again.

On the 16th the movement continued against the enemy, their sharpshooters annoying the battery boys constantly. Two of the horses in the battery were wounded. The 18th the battery was moved forward a short distance, and works were thrown up for the guns. Some shells were thrown towards Kenesaw, thinking that they reached the crest, but we afterward found that the distance was too great for them to reach, thus showing the deception common to people that are raised in level countries. The morning of the 19th found the enemy gone, having been flanked and forced to evacuate. One section of the battery was pushed forward and commenced firing at the rebels on the top of Kenesaw Mountain. During the forenoon the rest of the battery was placed in position to open on the mountain. The enemy's position at this time was as follows: Kenesaw was his strong point and salient; the left flank across Noonday Creek, and his right flank was across Nose Creek, both retired and supported by strong parapets.

On the 20th the battery moved to within 1400 yards of Big Kenesaw and opened fire.[15] At night the enemy constructed works on

15. The battery fired 600 rounds on the 19th and 702 rounds on the 20th.—*Barnett*, p. 829. Major General Jefferson C. Davis said: "The batteries of the division came into action [June 19], and during the remainder of the day contested the ground with good success. The troops were entrenched and field-works thrown up for the batteries during the night. The troops remained in this position with but little change until the night of the 25th, during which time sharp skirmishing frequently engaged the infantry, and fierce artillery contests sprang up between the contending batteries. In these encounters our batteries invariably manifested their superiority and discipline over that of the enemy."—"Report," *O. R.*, Series 1, Vol. 38, Part 1, p. 632.

the summit of the mountain, and on the 22nd, opened fire on the Union batteries in front of Kenesaw, and many duels were fought between the two lines. It was a very pretty sight to witness the flight of shells, to and fro, just as it was growing dark, with their streams of fire and lightning-like explosions. A line of thick and heavy bastions for four batteries was built on the night of the 22nd, into which the guns moved on the 23rd, the horses and caisons remaining back in the rear out of danger, as it was thought; but one morning a little after daylight, the rebels opened on the camp with their batteries, and made it so warm with exploding shells that for once a part of the battery "skedaddled" very lively to a place of safety in a thick piece of woods out of sight.

General Davis having discovered a rebel signal station on the highest point of the summit of Kenesaw, sent word to Captain Barnett to try his guns on the point. Corporal Ed. Smith, a gunner, was selected to give it a trial. The corporal after viewing the ground, thought he could not elevate his gun enough inside the bastion, so ran it outside, and giving it an elevation of about twenty-five degrees threw a percussion shell with such accuracy that it cut off a limb of the tree under which the enemy's signal men were working, causing them to scatter quickly. The second and third shells burst right among them, killing and wounding several of them. For such skillful work Captain Barnett promoted Corporal Smith to sergeant, he, prior to that time, having been acting sergeant of the gun. The following extract is from the correspondent of the *Chicago Tribune*, who was with the 14th Army Corps, dated June 24th, 1864.

Yesterday afternoon the rebels opened an extensive artillery fire from a battery placed on the top of Kenesaw Mountain, but it was soon silenced by Battery I, 2d Illinois Light Artillery, which did some of the best shooting your correspondent has yet seen. The sky was dark and cloudy, and as the shell burst over the rebel batteries, the flash could be seen, resembling a vivid streak of sharp forked lightning. The effect of each shell was to make the rebel gunners retire to a place of safety, from which

they would once in awhile run out and fire off
their pieces. But our boys had them in a tight
place and the shelling was so vigorously followed up that the rebels were obliged to retire
altogether.[16]

The 27th of June the battle of Kenesaw was fought, and met
with no beneficial result. It taught Sherman the lesson that it does
not pay to rush men against the well manned breastworks. The
battery occupied the position at the foot of Kenesaw in the heavy
bastions, and began firing at nine o'clock in the forenoon. A steady
fire was kept up, while the infantry was moving up the side of the
mountain, by the twenty-four guns in line with the battery. During
the bombardment Thomas Penniwell, acting as Number One on the
gun, had his right hand and lower portion of his arm torn off by the
premature discharge of the gun while ramming down a shell. Poor
Penniwell! How well do we remember what a time the Captain had
trying to make him take a team in Nashville, Tenn. He was
determined not to be a postillion, and claimed that he would not,
could not guide a horse, begging and pleading to remain a cannoneer, but the Captain was also determined that he should ride.
Penniwell could not get on, and when he was on fell off, to be put on
again, only to fall off as soon as left alone. Then two men held him
on, one at each leg, then he could not guide the horse, which ended
finally with three men working with him, one leading the horse, and
one on each side in which condition he rode around the battery, all
the while exclaiming: "It's no use, Captain, I just can't ride. I can't
be anything but a cannoneer." At last Tom gave in and took a team,
but made a very poor driver, and when complained of, always said,
"It's no use, Captain, I never will make a good postillion. It's no
use." Finally he was returned to the gun to be mustered out a crip-
ple for life.

---

16. This story, headed "An Artillery Fight" appears in the *Chicago
Tribune* of Saturday, July 2, 1864. The authors appear to have copied it
from *Woodruff*, p. 431; Woodruff did not copy accurately from the
Tribune, and his version agrees with the authors. The version above is as
originally printed in the *Tribune*.

A more or less constant fire was kept up on the enemy's batteries until the 2nd of July, when during the night they abandoned Kenesaw Mountain and evacuated their works in front of Sherman's lines. The battery joined the 2nd Division of the 14th Corps,[17] a short distance south of Kenesaw, opposite where the 2nd Brigade charged the rebel works. What a splendid charge they made! Right up to, and on to them they went. Colonel Dan McCook fell mortally wounded,[18] as he stood on top, leading his brigade, our old brigade, one we knew was true gold, and as fully to be trusted. That body of men dug themselves into the ground not more than a hundred feet from the rebel breastworks, and held there till the line was evacuated, fighting "tooth and nail," till trees eighteen inches through were literally cut down with minnie [Minié] bullets. Balls of fire were thrown between the lines by both sides to keep either party from charging at night. Tunnels were started and were nearly completed when evacuation took place. That was Dan McCook's brigade on which Battery I banked all of her capital.

On the 3rd the division passed through Marrietta [Marietta], Ga., and the Union troops came up with the enemy strongly entrenched at Smyrna Church, five miles from Marietta. The battery was sent to the front and placed in position early on the 4th of July, and celebrated that glorious day by firing over one-hundred rounds of shell into the rebel lines. An amusing event took place here, which may be worth telling. The men of the battery were set to work building bastions for the guns. The morning was hot, the ground hard, but they worked faithfully till about nine o'clock with the rebel breastworks in plain view, which showed a battery bearing directly on our position, and every moment it was expected that it would open to prevent the building of Union works; but lack of ammunition saved the boys from molestation, as it did many times on the Atlanta Campaign. The Captain owned a dog which was named Rosecrans, in honor of our old commander. It had a very bad and dangerous habit of chasing the battery shells as dogs do stones when thrown for sport, which habit finally cost him his life in

17. In July the Battery was transferred from the artillery of the 2nd Division, 14th Corps, to the artillery Brigade, 14th Corps, in which it would serve to the end of the war.

front of Atlanta through the viciousness of a rebel sharpshooter.

The boys exhausted with their toil and the heat, thought that a good cool glass of lemonade would rejuvinate their spirits and refresh the inner man. Lemons were procured from a sutler in the rear, and by contributions from the sugar sacks of the boys a fine pailful was prepared. A tall leafy oak tree furnished shade as it overhung the breastworks which being elevated above the ground gave chance for the cool breeze to sweep gently about their fevered brows. All were enjoying themselves to the greatest extent on top of the works, when the Captain observed that the rebel gunners could have no better target than that crowd presented. No sooner was the word spoken than there was a puff of white smoke from the embrasure of the rebel fort. No sooner seen than there were many heels twinkling in the air, and many forms were mixed on the ground behind the breastworks, with a yelping dog scared at the sudden change of base, and a lot of blinking, winking men who were expecting every second to feel pieces of shell tearing their way through their vitals. But one, braver than the rest, put his head above the works to take observations, and found that the rebel gun had fired in the opposite direction, and our battery had had no cause for alarm. Of course there was much laughter and joking over the event while the boys went on with their work.

In the afternoon the battery was moved out of the works and taken still farther to the front, which position, it seems, was in front of one of the divisions of Hooker's Corps. The battery opened, firing to the right and front, but had not fired many rounds, when there came a volley of caseshot from the batteries of Hooker's Corps, fairly raking the ground in our immediate front, some pieces tearing their way through our battery. In the meantime Sherman with his staff had taken a position of observation a little to the left, but was in range of the fire of Hooker's batteries. As soon as he found out what was the matter he sent for Hooker, and one of the orderlies told that Hooker got one of the worst cursings from Sherman that he ever heard; that Hooker told Sherman that he was ready to take his corps

18. Colonel Daniel McCook was mortally wounded in the attack on Kenesaw Mountain June 27, and died July 17, having been promoted to Brigadier General the day before his death.

and charge the rebels at any time to show that he was not afraid to be at the front, as Sherman intimated that Hooker did not know how far his line was from that of the enemy. Hooker soon left Sherman's army,[19] as there had been previous trouble between them. Later in the day the battery returned to its first position and shelled the line in front of that point, as there was an advance of the skirmish line to determine whether the rebels were there in force, which was shown conclusively by the heavy fire from the whole rebel line.

During that night the "Johnies" left their works and fell back to the line of entrenchments on the north side of the Chattahoochee River. The battery advanced with the division to a position not far from the Marietta road where it went into camp, after taking a position near a railroad bridge and shelling the rebels for a couple of hours. From this high position near Vining [or Vining's] Station, the spires of the churches in Atlanta could be seen plainly, and it made every heart rejoice to be able to see the goal of a long arduous campaign. Here again Sherman's "flanking machine" was put in motion, under command of [Major] General [John M.] Schofield, of the 23rd Corps, who crossed the Chattahoochee at Paice's [Pace's] Ferry, near the mouth of Soap Creek, and began operation against the enemy's flank, compelling him to evacuate his works on the north side of the Chattahoochee on the 9th of July. The battery was still in position throwing shells into their works, when they fell back across the river. At night all traces of the rebels left the north side and gave Sherman full possession of the right bank of the Chattahoochee with Atlanta only eight miles distant. The battery laid in camp near the river, and some of the guns were used in shelling the rebs on the south side the next day after the evacuation. While in this camp a little event transpired that will show the discipline of the battery.

19. After the death on July 22 of Major General James B. McPherson, Sherman had to find another officer to command the Army of the Tennessee. He chose Major General Oliver O. Howard, and Major General Joseph Hooker, believing he should have had the position, asked to be relieved of command. His request was granted and he was assigned to command the Northern Department, where he was when the war ended. Unquestionably Sherman did not get along well with Hooker.—See *Sherman*, Vol. 2, pp. 85–86. See also Francis F. McKinney *Education in*

At Nashville, Tenn., there was a little wild Irishman came as a recruit to the battery, and will be remembered as coming to his first roll call with a chunk of soft bread in one hand and a fistful of cold boiled meat in the other. He was a good brave soldier, but a little slouchy in his dress, and would persist in wearing his cap on the back of his head with the hair hanging over his eyes. It happened that he was on guard when Lieutenant Coe was officer of the day, who came along where the Irishman was pacing his beat, cap on the back of his head as usual. The Lieutenant told him to put his cap on right, and received the reply: "Be gorry, sir, me cap is me own, and I'll do what I plaze wid it. So I will." The Lieutenant repeated the command, and received the same reply. Then the lieutenant called the guard and ordered them to take the Irishman and put a rail on his back and see that he carried it till he was ready to obey commands. The Irishman carried the rail all that day, and the next, always replying to the query if he was ready to obey orders: "Be gorry, sir, me cap is me own, and I'll do what I like wid it." The next day he began to weaken, and finally sent for Lieutenant Coe, and as soon as the lieutenant came, he threw down his rail with a very polite bow, and neatly placing his cap in the required position, said: "I beg yer pardon, yer honor, I'd be no gintlman at all, at all, if I did not pay attintion to the opinion of so foine a gintleman, as ye are. Sure, lieutenant, ye're right, and I'm in the wrong intirely." "All right," said Lieutenant Coe, "if that is the way you feel, you can go to your quarters and report for duty."

July 16th the battery received new guns,[20] and on the 17th marched to Pace's Ferry, five miles above the railroad bridge over the Chattahoochee and crossed over to the Atlanta side with part of the 2nd Division, pushing on towards Peach Tree Creek, doing a little skirmishing in the afternoon.[21] On the 19th the battery took

Violence. The Life of George H. Thomas and the History of the Army of the Cumberland (Detroit: Wayne State University Press, 1961), pp. 351–52. Hooker was succeeded by Major General Henry W. Slocum. This work will be cited hereafter as *Thomas*.

20. *Woodruff*, p. 432, says the guns were inspected and condemned, each having fired over twelve-hundred rounds in the Atlanta Campaign.

21. On July 17 General John B. Hood succeeded Johnston as commander of the Confederate troops.

position on the bank of the creek, but did not have much to do in the battle of Peach Tree, which was fought that day. The extreme left of the rebel line was opposite the battery's position, and a few shells thrown at the skirmish line, also at a house in which some sharpshooters were posted, was all that fell to the lot of Battery I. In the afternoon the battery crossed the creek on a bridge of driftwood lodged in the stream, and had a chance to examine the effect of the shells thrown into the house, which must have made it very warm for the sharpshooters. On the 22nd, (the day General McPherson, commanding the 15th and 17th Corps, was killed in the battle on the left of Atlanta) the battery marched a short distance to the front and right, and found the enemy strongly entrenched around Atlanta. On the 23rd the men built works for the guns, and tried some very long shots at the city, which we never knew how far they went, as no one ever reported where they fell.

On the 27th the division moved to a position on Procter's Creek, and on the 28th it was ordered to the right, General James D. Morgan in command, as General Davis was sick. General Sherman in his *Memoirs* says: "As General Jeff. C. Davis's division was, as it were, left out of the line, I ordered it on the evening before to march down to Turner's Ferry, and then to take a road laid down on the maps, which led from there toward East Point, ready to engage any enemy that might attack our general right flank on the 28th. The plan failed on account of the division taking the wrong road, thus causing great delay." [22] The truth of the matter was that the division went farther than was needful, and it took too long to get back to the flank, though it may have taken the wrong road or been delayed by the enemy's cavalry, as [Major] General [Oliver O.] Howard says in his description.

As the writer remembers the movement, the division marched on the Sandtown road to the right, till near noon, then rested till about one o'clock when the division started to return, moving sometimes on roads and sometimes through fields. About five o'clock a few rebel

22. The correct quotation, taken from the Indiana University Press edition of Sherman's *Memoirs*, Vol. 2, p. 88, follows: "As General Jeff. C. Davis's division was, as it were, left out of line, I ordered it on the evening before to march down toward Turner's Ferry, and then to

cavalry made their appearance on the right flank of the moving column, and fired a number of shots, but the delay was not more than ten minutes, or just long enough to throw out a company of infantry as flankers. About sundown the division arrived near enough to Logan's flank to hear the volleys of musketry, and did not get on to the field until about dark, when the battle was all over.

Probably Dr. J. R. Bedford of Verona, Ill. will long remember that evening for the incident that happened to him. As soon as the battery camped men went in different directions for wood and water. It was Bedford's turn to go for water, so, taking a camp kettle, he started out in search of a spring. He had not been gone long, when he rushed back with the palor of death on his face, exclaiming, "Oh my god! oh my god!" acting more like an insane person, while it was impossible to find out what was the matter. After awhile he quieted down enough to tell the circumstance. It seems that he went down into a ravine among some thick brush, thinking there might be a spring in the low ground. As he was hunting he stepped on something that was soft, and which at the same time gave a gurgle then a squawk. Stooping down to discover the cause of the sound he put his hand onto the cold, clammy face of a dead man who had that day been shot in a charge on the Union line. Bounding out of the ravine he ran to the battery, panting like one stricken with most perfect demoralization. It was his first experience on a battle field among the dead, as he came to the battery as a young recruit, when it was on veteran furlough; but he made one of the bravest and best of soldiers.

The battle of Ezra Church or the battle on the right of Atlanta, to distinguish it from the battle on the left, was fought between two corps of the rebel army, Hardee's and [Lieutenant General Stephen D.] Lee's, and [Major General John A.] Logan's and [Major General Francis P.] Blair's of the Union. It began about eleven o'clock in the forenoon, and ended substantially by four in the afternoon, in the complete repulse of the rebels, they leaving about

take a road laid down on our maps which led from there toward East Point, ready to engage any enemy that might attack our general right flank, after the same manner as had been done to the left flank on the 22d."

one thousand dead on the field. It was a great disappointment to General Sherman that the division under [Brigadier] General [James D.] Morgan did not arrive in time to take the rebel line in the flank. He says: "At no instant of time did I feel the least uneasiness about the result on the 28th, but wanted to reap fuller results, hoping that Davis's division would come up at the instant of defeat, and catch the enemy in flank, but the woods were dense, the roads obscure, and as usual this division got on the wrong road, and did not come into position until about dark." [23]

On the morning of the 29th, after the hard day's march before, the 2nd Division advanced the line of battle, and the battery went into position at the front. On the 30th the division moved to the right, advancing the lines and taking position. On the 31st the battery, with the division, made a reconnaissance to the right, returning to their old position at night after a disagreeable march, it having rained nearly all day. [24] Sherman in his *Memoirs* says: [25]

> The month of August opened hot and sultry, but our position before Atlanta was healthy, with ample supply of wood, water, and provisions. The troops had become habituated to the slow and steady progress of the siege; the skirmish lines were held close up to the enemy, were covered by rifle-trenches or logs, and kept up a continuous clatter of musketry. The main lines were held farther back, adapted to the shape of the ground, with muskets loaded and stacked for instant use. The

23. Howard mentions Morgan's Division, but does not say that it took the wrong road or had been held up by enemy cavalry.—See Oliver O. Howard, *Autobiography*, 2 vols. (New York: Baker & Taylor Company, 1907), Vol. 2, pp. 20–25. See also *Sherman*, Vol. 2, p. 91. *Thomas*, p. 355, states that General James D. Morgan led the Division that day and that there were two roads where Sherman only knew of one; Morgan took the one unknown to Sherman, and does not deserve this censure.
24. Throughout the month of August, 38 enlisted men from the 2nd Independent Battery, Minnesota Light Artillery, were detached to serve with Battery I.
25. *Sherman*, Vol. 2, p. 96.
26. Major General John M. Palmer claimed he was at least equal in rank to Major General John M. Schofield and refused to serve under his command. Sherman listened to both men and decided Schofield ranked Palmer, because Schofield's commission as Brigadier bore an earlier date. Palmer disagreed and offered his resignation, which Thomas and Sherman agreed should be accepted. Palmer then resigned his position as commander of the 14th Corps and returned to Illinois. This altercation

field-batteries were in select positions, covered by handsome parapets, and occasional shots from them gave life and animation to the scene. The men loitered about the trenches carelessly, or busied themselves in constructing ingenious huts out of abundant timber, and seemed as snug, comfortable, and happy as though they were at home. . . . Two divisions of the Fourteenth Corps (Baird's and Jeff. C. Davis's) were detached to the right rear, and held in reserve.

August 4th [Major] General [John M.] Palmer, commanding the 14th Corps, was ordered to report to General Schofield by command of General Sherman, but refused to serve under him. After a sharp controversy between Sherman, Thomas, and Palmer, Palmer was relieved, and General Jeff. C. Davis of the 2nd Division, was assigned to the command. Much as Palmer was liked by the rank and file, they had a very poor opinion of his patriotism after this display of over-sensitiveness.[26]

There was a continual swinging of the right flank to get on the West Point railroad. The lines of breastworks showed the radiating circle of the right wing of the army, and Battery I was not far from the right of the turning point. Finally on the 7th of August the battery took an exposed position on the skirmish line where more men were wounded and killed than any other place during the campaign.[27] The enemy's skirmish line was about five hundred yards in front, in plain sight. Strong bastions were built by the men, thick

did not affect his civil career, for he was elected governor in 1867 and later served as U.S. Senator. He was succeeded by Brigadier General Jefferson C. Davis on August 22nd; Davis was succeeded as commander of the 2nd Division by Brigadier General James D. Morgan.

27. Colonel John G. Mitchell in his "Report," O. R., Series I, Vol. 38, Part 1, p. 681, says: "August 7, advanced skirmishers and captured lines of rifle-pits, prisoners, arms, &c.; during the night intrenched Seventy-eighth Illinois and Barnett's battery on picket line within 300 yards of the enemy's works. August 8, 9, 10, and 11, General appearance unchanged; firing constant."

Lt. Colonel Maris R. Vernon, commanding 78th Illinois, stated, O. R., Series I, Vol. 38, Part 1, p. 689: "Again, on the 8th, at 11 P.M., the regiment advanced to a position in front of the main line and erected works supporting Captain Barnett's battery, in sight of the enemy's lines, and within short range of four of his heavy forts, mounting from four to six guns. The regiment was relieved from this position on the evening of the 10th and ordered back to the second line of works."

enough to resist shell, with deep embrasures. The two sections occupied separate positions, one facing a six-gun Napoleon battery to the right, and the other a section of six-pound smooth bores directly in front. For the first two or three days in this position the enemy's skirmish line kept up a perfect shower of lead most of the time, trying to silence the battery, but they did not succeed, while the gunners knocked their head logs onto the poor rebs in the ditches, till they begged for an armistice, and promised not to shoot if the battery would not. One morning two rebel sharpshooters took a position in a rifle pit to the left of the section on their right, and commenced to enfilade the inside of the bastions regardless of the armistice. Lieutenant Coe mounted the breastworks and shouted over to the "Johnies," wanting to know why they had broken the agreement. They said that they could not prevent the two from shooting, and that the battery should punish them for breaking the armistice. A gun was taken out of the bastion and aimed at the rifle-pit. The shell went too high and struck just beyond. "A leetle too high, Yanks," shouted the "Johnies." The next shot struck in front of the pit, when the "Johnies" shouted, "A leetle too low, Yanks." In the meantime the two sharpshooters were doing their best to silence the gun, but their aim was confused from some cause, and no harm was done in the battery. The next shell went into the pit and that was the last of those fellows, while the "Johnies" shouted, "That's the time ye did it. Bully for you!"

The horses and caisons were kept back a mile in the rear out of danger. All the cooking was done there till the armistice was established, and all the non-combatants slept there most of the time. Every gun was loaded at night to be ready for attacks at a moment's notice. One Sunday morning a shirt was seen stretched across the embrasure of the rebel bastion in front. The Captain took it to be a challenge and opened on it. The rebel guns returned the fire till they were dismounted and their bastions were badly torn to pieces. Orders were sent to the other section on the left to open fire on the six-gun Napoleon battery. The little Rodmans spit away at them for a number of rounds when all at once six shells came answering back the challenge, and a deadly duel had begun not to end till three men were killed, and one man mortally wounded, and three badly hurt. The fight was kept up till late in the afternoon, the section firing a half hour after the rebel battery had stopped, probably not silenced, but for want of ammunition, for that condition more often silenced rebel batteries than Union marksmanship, to speak without bombast. Right in the rear of the section were about six hundred new recruits for Minnesota regiments, which had not been distributed yet, these received all the shells that passed over the breastworks, giving them a pretty severe "baptism of fire." C. [Christian G.] Geyer was wounded at this time, August 9th, and died in the hospital at Chattanooga, of gangrene, September 18th, '64. John Riley, John Linn, William Haines, and Miller were wounded. Ole Oleson, a detailed man from a Minnesota regiment, was killed by a piece of shell striking him in the head, and passing partly through his body. William McAllister was wounded the 7th, the day the battery moved into position, through the thigh, while Meyers [Charles P. Myers or Meyers] and a Norwegian detailed to the battery [probably Peter Streicher] was badly wounded a few days later, the first through the front of the stomach, and the second through the bowels, which caused his death three hours after. The same bullet hit both men, just as the gun was fired it came through the embrasure.[28] Meyers and Geyer were artisans, the first was the battery blacksmith, and the second the harness maker, before the boys veteranized, but they would not take those positions after they re-enlisted.

One day, a little after noon, while the men, most of them, were snoozing in the shade, and everything was quiet, who should come into the battery but General Sherman on foot, attended by only one orderly, his neck-tie awry, and in his usual undress uniform, looking more like a common officer of the day. He did not [want] anyone disturbed, and after spying around a short time went his way down the line of works.

During the time the battery was in front of Atlanta, for

---

28. "August 7, built works for the guns, about 8 miles southwest of Atlanta, and was engaged every day up to the 26th, having 2 men killed, 8 wounded, and 1 horse killed."—*Barnett*, p. 830.

twenty one days, it was under fire most of that period, exposed to infantry and artillery duels.[29] In front of the battery, at this position, there was a cool spring of water, about equidistant between the lines. The men in the front lines of the army agreed upon a truce, that they might go to the spring to drink of its fresh sparkling water and fill their canteens. Several of the boys belonging to the 31st Ohio infantry, after negotiating with some of the "Johnies" at the spring, would wear blouses double so that when the "Rebs" met them again the boys would give each one an extra blouse and thus the "Reb" would go with the Union men into their line and there would be turned over the provost marshal of the brigade. This scheme was kept up for a time till the rebel officers got a knowledge of it, when they put a stop to their men coming to the spring. Sergeant Ed. Smith came very near being taken prisoner by a rebel while he was alone at the spring; but just as the fellow drew his revolver and demanded his surrender, he sprang upon him and knocked him down, taking him prisoner, and then marched him inside our lines.

On the night of the 26th, about ten o'clock, the battery moved out of the breastworks, and marched to Utoy Creek. A thunder storm was coming up in the west, which made the darkness profound. In the midst of the movement the rebels opened with their artillery, the streams of fire from the fuses of the shells, the roar of the thunder and the explosions of cannons, made the occasion one long to be remembered, especially to the person who tried to dodge the streaming, shrieking shell that seemed to be making directly towards him from the mouth of a rebel gun.[30]

The 28th the division marched to the West Point Railroad and commenced tearing it up, burning the ties and bending the rails, and

---

29. Brigadier General Jefferson C. Davis complimented the Battery and Captain Barnett and Lt. Coe in his report, *O. R.*, Series I, Vol. 38, Part 1, p. 637: "The artillery attached to this division consisted of Battery I, Second Illinois Light Artillery, and the Fifth Wisconsin Battery. The efficiency, discipline, and good conduct on the march and in battle of both officers and men was in the highest degree commendable. Capt. Charles M. Barnett, chief of artillery, proved himself a skillful and energetic officer by his excellent management of his batteries throughout the campaign. Captain Gardner and Lieutenant Coe, battery com-

thoroughly destroying the track. The battery in going into camp in the afternoon was fired on by a squad of rebel cavalry, who fled immediately, as soon as skirmishers were thrown out to meet them. The next day was spent in tearing up the railroad, and the 30th the division moved toward the Macon and Western Railroad. The cornfields were just in season for roasting ears, and the men were hungry for something fresh and green, so the camp kettles were kept busy in cooking night and day. One of the boys ate sixteen ears before quitting and the surgeon worked with him the rest of the night to save his life from over-eating. The following incident is taken from Sherman's *Memoirs*,[31] speaking of this march.

We stopped for a short noon-rest near a little church (marked on our maps as Shoal Creek Church, which stood back about a hundred yards from the road, in a grove of native oaks. The infantry column had halted in the road, stacked their arms, and the men were scattered about—some lying in the shade of the trees, and others were bringing corn-stalks from a large cornfield across the road to feed our horses, while still others had arms full of roasting ears, then in their prime. Hundreds of fires were soon started with the fence-rails, and the men were busy roasting the ears. Thomas and I were walking up and down the road which led to the church, discussing the chances of the movement, which he thought were extra-hazardous, and our path carried us by a fire at which a soldier was roasting his corn. The fire was built artistically; the man was stripping the ears of their husks, standing them in front of his fire, watching them carefully, and turning each ear little by little, so as to roast it nicely. He was down on his knees intent on his business, paying little heed to the stately and serious deliberations of his leaders. Thomas's mind was running on the

manders, performed their duties ably and efficiently. Their batteries are among the best in the service."

30. The "Return of Battery I, 2nd Reg't of Arty for the month of August, 1864" reported that on August 9 one Battery man and one detailed man were wounded; on August 10, one battery man; on August 11, one battery man severely wounded and one detailed man mortally wounded; from August 19 to 21, one battery man severely and two slightly wounded and one detailed man wounded and one killed.

31. *Sherman*, Vol. 2, pp. 106–7.

fact that we had cut loose from our base of supplies, and that seventy thousand men were then dependent for their food on the chance supplies of the country (already impoverished by the requisitions of the enemy), and on the contents of our wagons. Between Thomas and his men there existed a most kindly relation, and he frequently talked with them in the most familiar way. Pausing awhile, and watching the operations of this man roasting his corn he said, "What are you doing?" The man looked up smilingly: "Why General, I am laying in a supply of provisions." "That is right my man, but don't waste your provisions." As we resumed our walk, the man remarked, in a sort of musing way, but loud enough for me to hear: "There he goes, there goes the old man, economizing as usual. "Economizing" with corn, which cost only the labor of gathering and roasting!"

The 31st a part of Fourteenth Corps struck the Macon road near Rough and Ready, while the Army of the Tennessee under Howard, reached it at Jonesboro, and immediately threw up works which were soon attacked by Hardee's corps, which attack was easily repulsed.

The morning of the 1st of September was a beautiful one, and the division started early towards Jonesboro. The advance had not gone far before they struck a detachment of rebels, and there was a sharp little skirmish in which one of the enemy was killed and left on the ground to be viewed by the troops as they marched past. He was a man about six feet six inches in height and of fine build, and looked more like a dead giant as he lay there face down, arms thrown forward, probably as he fell when he was shot. About noon the division reached the left of the 15th corps, but right in front was a low swampy piece of ground covered with long coarse grass. This the battery had to move around towards the right, which brought them in rear of the 15th corps, then it had to move to the left to gain a hill east of the low ground, on which to post the battery. There was constant skirmishing going on in front of the 15th corps, which, with the booming of the artillery, made war music for the marching columns to step to in moving to their positions. Again had the division struck rebel works which were in plain view. Down hill to the east, over a small stream, up a gentle rise, covered by a cornfield were rebel breastworks, running nearly north and south. In the direct front was a rebel battery (Swett's Mississippi,) of four guns.[32] Battery I opened on it, and soon it replied, the duel lasting for a half-hour. It is now nearly four o'clock, and the division has moved down into the cornfield, preparing for a charge. Our old brigade is there, and will for the first time move under the eye of her battery. The first brigade is to the left of the battery, the third is in reserve. The Fifth Wisconsin battery is to the right in a hollow, and has an enfilading fire on the rebel line, which is telling so well that Swett's battery turns most of its attention that way. Battery I now moves farther to the left on to higher ground that overlooks the whole field, and will give the boys a splendid view of the coming charge. Again the battery opens on the Mississippi battery. See, there goes a caison into the air! Ah, two of their guns are down, while their infantry is hugging the breastworks to save themselves. Things are getting intensely interesting. It is after four, nearly five o'clock. The sun is getting low in the west. Oh heavens! See! The Union line begins to move. Faster, faster, forward with a rush and a yell go the red capped New York Zouaves [17th New York Veteran Volunteer Infantry] on the left, straight for the rebel works. Ah, see that line of red fire shoot out from the breastworks, and see that line of red uniforms melt, falling forward, downward, and backward, with only a short waver, than like a tornado over the works it goes, and the graybacked "Johnies" come to our side. But look! There goes our brigade, the old 2nd, with lines as even as when they played sham battle with Battery I in Nashville; with guns at charge and never a shot, they walk over that line of works in spite of canister of Minié balls. How Dan McCook would have cheered and danced to have seen his brigade make that charge, but his spirit led them, for had he not drilled his pride and ambition into them while leading them from Louisville to Kenesaw. The "Johnies" jump to our side of the works,

32. This was presumably the Mississippi battery commanded by Lieutenant H. Shannon, of Hotchkiss's Battalion of Artillery, of Lt. General William J. Hardee's Corps. There is a good description of this action in the "Report" of Brigadier General James D. Morgan, O. R., Series I, Vol. 38, Part 1, pp. 641–42.

and come running, yelling, and swearing towards the battery. 'Tis the same [Brigadier General Daniel C.] Govan's brigade that faced us at Chickamauga,[33] and now this is the end of them for the war; for they can not be exchanged in time to do much more fighting. How the boys cheer and throw up their hats, shake hands, embrace and howl for joy! Yes, this is glorious war, that charge and the "boys in blue" the victors. Battery I must go forward to help our brave infantrymen, and Captain Barnett along with Major Houghtaling, spurs to the front, but hold, Sherman says that Davis must stay the Fourteenth Corps till Howard can send his divisions to the east and south of Jonesboro, while [Major] General [David S.] Stanley, with the Fourth, and General Schofield with the Twenty-Third Corps, can swing around on the left, and thus "bag" General Hardee. Sable night travels faster than can the men through brush and woods so thick and roads so dim, and Hardee is too fleet of foot.

Eight guns and over two thousand prisoners were the trophies of this victory and failure. Failure because the whole of Hardee's corps should have been captured, which would have been the result, if Sherman had had two hours more to have maneuvered. The battery camped that night on the battlefield, and the next day moved into Jonesboro. In the night there was sound of battle in the vicinity of the city of Atlanta, which was thought at first to be an attack of [General John B.] Hood on the Twentieth Corps at the river; but before night, the 2nd, the glad news came that Atlanta was evacuated, and the "goal" was won at last. Again there was great joy, and every soul thought that it was that much nearer home.

A little incident occurred at Jonesboro, which illustrates one phase of a soldier's life. Close by the camp of the battery there was a very fine house containing a large library and a nice piano, all of which belonged to a rank rebel who had fled with Hardee's troops. The boys needed boards to build floors for their tents, so first the blinds and then the doors were taken, then the siding began to disappear, finally the whole house was used, piece by piece till naught was left. In the meantime there were some very good piano

33. Brigadier General Daniel C. Govan's Brigade was in Major General Patrick R. Cleburne's Division of Hardee's Corps.

players went to the instrument and gave the boys some piano music to which there were soon men waltzing and dancing the schottische, and at last there were three or four quadrilles "tripping the light fantastic too." The house began to shake and weave, which showed danger to the dancers, and many began to run out of the building for safety. "What shall we do with the piano?" said one. "It is shame to have so fine an instrument crushed," said another. "Let us take it to the house across the street," says the third. "Agreed," says the fourth, and so with many willing hands the piano was lifted and carried over the way. A knock at the door, and a scared, scowling face appeared and inquired what was wanted. The errand was told and permission was given to leave the piano, then the best player sat down to the instrument, and all the boys joined in singing *The Star Spangled Banner, Yankee Doodle,* and *America;* then bowing politely they all left the house never to enter it again; but left a little incident in the history of that family that probably will be handed down to future generations.

On the 6th the battery, with the division, moved back towards Atlanta as far as Rough and Ready, and camped in the rain which continued all night, but hearts so light over the glad victory could not be affected by any dampness of the weather. The next day, marched to near Atlanta, and the next entered the suburbs where the battery expected to stay for awhile.

Thus was brought to a close one of the greatest and grandest campaigns ever recorded in history. Battery I felt proud to think that all through the long campaign it had done its duty bravely and well, taking part in the engagements at Tunnel Hill, Buzzard Roost, Resaca, Rome, Ga., Dallas, Big Shanty, Kenesaw Mountain, Peach Tree Creek, Atlanta and Jonesboro. It was under fire, more or less, nearly every day from the start to the finish, and expended 6,766 rounds of ammunition, mostly of shell and case shot, fire at long range as only once was canister used and that at Dallas.

Upon arriving at Atlanta the men were not allowed much rest, but were set to work building arbors, policing camp and grubbing stumps, as the officers thought it necessary to keep the men busy all the time. But they were not kept long at camp drudgery, as General Hood thought it would be a good time to attack Sherman's rear, and march on to Nashville.[34]

On the 28th the battery received marching orders, and on the 29th two sections, with their equipments, took the cars, and went north with the 2nd Division under the command of General Morgan, leaving one section, and the rest of the baggage in camp in charge of Quartermaster Sergeant Brown and Sergeant Smith, Major Houghtaling was temporarily assigned to the command of the artillery in and around Nashville, Tenn., and Captain Barnett put in as Acting Chief of Artillery of the 14th Corps. The two sections of the battery, with Captain Barnett, and Lieutenant Coe and Lieutenant Rich, arrived at Chattanooga, September 30th, at eleven in the afternoon. October 1st they proceeded by cars to Stephenson, Ala., and from there to Huntsville, where they arrived at seven o'clock at night, where the battery unloaded from the train. The following is taken from an article in the *Century Magazine*, written by Henry Stone.[35]

On September 28th, 1864, less than four weeks from the day the Union forces occupied Atlanta, General Sherman, who found his still unconquered enemy, General Hood, threatening his communications in Georgia, and that formidable raider, General Forrest, playing mischief in West Tennessee, sent to the latter state two divisions—General Newton's of the Fourth Corps, and General J. D. Morgan's of the Fourteenth—to aid in destroying, if possible, that intrepid dragoon. To make assurance doubly sure, the next day he ordered General

34. After abandoning Atlanta, Hood stopped at Lovejoy's Station, then moved to the west, to Palmetto; there were Confederate command changes, one of them bringing General Pierre G. T. Beauregard from the east to be Hood's nominal superior. Confederate cavalry was active behind Sherman; so he sent Major General John Newton's 2nd Division of the 4th Corps to Chattanooga and Brigadier General John M. Corse's 2nd Division of the 17th Corps to Rome. After Hood left Palmetto, Sherman sent Thomas on September 29 with Brigadier General James B. Morgan's 2nd Division of the 14th Corps to Tennessee. Sherman left the 20th Corps, Major General Henry W. Slocum, in Atlanta, and with his remaining troops set out north after Hood. The army, however, was much changed: Army of the Ohio (23rd Corps), Major General Jacob D. Cox; Army of the Cumberland, Major General David S. Stanley (4th Corps), Major General Jefferson C. Davis, 14th Corps; Army of the Tennessee,

George H. Thomas, his most capable and experienced lieutenant, and commander of more than three-fifths of his grand army, "back to Stephenson and Dechard . . . to look to Tennessee. . . . The task of expelling Forrest and reopening the broken communications was speedily completed."

On the 24th of September General Forrest captured Athens with over a thousand prisoners, and threatened the line of railroad in Tennessee. Afterwards he appeared before Huntsville and demanded the surrender of the place, but it was not conceded. He then moved to Athens which had been regarrisoned, and being closely pursued he had to turn back into Alabama, and cross the Tennessee River. Battery I took part in this pursuit; so on October 2nd the battery was again loaded onto the cars, and started for Athens; but about three miles from Huntsville the track was found torn up and the telegraph down. It took the troops all night to repair the road, and at daylight the train moved on to within three miles of Athens, where the battery unloaded on an improvised platform made out of a woodpile, and marched to the town and camped there that night, Forrest having decamped.

During the night while waiting for the troops to repair the railroad the train stopped where two large woodpiles had been burned by Forrest's cavalry, which were then two rows or beds of living coals on both sides of the track. It was a very comfortable place for a cool night, though a little dangerous for a train loaded with so much explosive material. The Commissary Sergeant issued some fresh beef to the men, long after dark, which was in the quarter, and the axes and saws were all packed away snugly, so the

Major General Oliver O. Howard, 15th Corps, Major General Peter J. Osterhaus and 17th Corps, Major General Thomas E. G. Ransom. Brigadier General Washington L. Elliott commanded the cavalry, of two divisions, headed by Brigadier General Hugh J. Kilpatrick and Brigadier General Kenner Garrard.

Sherman would chase Hood, never bringing him to bay; for all practical purposes, Sherman's pursuit of Hood ended at Gaylesville. Already decided to march from Atlanta to the sea (Savannah), Sherman sent Stanley's 4th Corps and Major General John M. Schofield's 23rd Corps to Thomas at Nashville. Sherman would turn his back on Hood; Thomas was to deal with Hood. Battery I went north with the 2nd Division after Hood and then returned to Atlanta to march to the sea. 35. This quotation appears in an article by Henry Stone, titled "Repelling Hood's Invasion of Tennessee" in B. & L., Vol. 4, p. 440.

boys had to cut up the meat as best they could with their pocket knives. A rib would be disected out, then laid on the live coals where it would broil nicely, then two men would sit down side by side and gnaw along the bone, back and forth, till it was picked clean. In the morning each man showed a streak of [black] from ear to ear where the broiled meat had slid round on the face.

On the 4th the division started for Florence, Ala., and arrived at Elk River about three o'clock in the afternoon, finding it very high from recent rains, but crossed it by a ford, though the current was so swift that the men could hardly keep their feet while wading. The division camped at Rogersville, about twenty four miles from Florence, in a violent rainstorm. The next day the roads were muddy, but moved out of camp at six o'clock, towards the river expecting to find Forrest. The 6th a detachment was sent to within one mile of Florence without any result, but distant cannonading was heard at the front. The camp at this time was near the Tennessee River, with the object of preventing Forrest from crossing, his camp being on the opposite side of the Shoals. There was some skirmishing across, by the infantrymen and Forrest's cavalry, but late in the afternoon on the 8th the division moved to Florence. Forrest thinking that the division was still in camp near the river, posted a battery opposite, and commenced a furious shelling of a deserted camp, during a violent thunder storm. The boys could not tell which it was, the thunder or cannon, till the next morning, when some stragglers came into camp and told how they had stopped at the old camp when the shelling began, and what a time they had had in dodging the shells, while the division was lying in perfect security at Florence. In the meantime Hood started his forces for the railroad in the rear of Atlanta, followed by Sherman on the 3rd of October to Smyrna Camp, and the next two days took him to Kenesaw Mountain from which he witnessed the fight at Allatoona between [Brigadier] General [John M.] Corse and [Major] General [Samuel G.] French of Hood's army. From thence Sherman followed Hood, "hither and thither," till he reached the vicinity of Gaylesville, on the 21st of October.

On the 10th of October the 2nd Division commenced its return to

Chattanooga over the same route it came, and arrived there on the 14th, where it remained in camp till the 18th. The 16th Sherman telegraphed to General Thomas at Nashville: [36] "Send me Morgan's and Newton's old divisions. Re-establish the road, and I will follow Hood wherever he may go. I think he will move to Blue Mountain. We can maintain our men and animals on the country." General Thomas's reply was: "Nashville, October 17th, 1864.—10:30 A.M. Schofield, whom I placed in command of the two divisions (Wagner's and Morgan's), was to move up Lookout Valley this A.M., to intercept Hood, should he be marching for Bridgeport. I will order him to join you with the two divisions, and will reconstruct the road as soon as possible."

October 18th the division marched for Gaylesville, out past the old camp at Rossville, over the Chickamauga battlefield, through Lafayette and Alpine, foraging on the way, arriving there about the 22nd, and camping there till the 28th, when the army started to return to Atlanta. The battery camped on the old battle ground at Rome [October 30–31], and while there one of the postillions led his team over a concealed well, the covering of which giving away the horses fell into the well, and nearly carried the driver with them. There was no way of getting them out, so they were shot to death in the well. Sherman now decided to cut loose from his base of supplies and start for the sea. The matter began to be talked over by the men, most of whom were strongly in favor of the move, feeling and knowing that it would be a "picnic."

At Cartersville the boys received from Uncle Sam a payment in fresh new "greenbacks," and also the battery got a new supply of horses from the quartermaster of the corps. Captain [Barnett] here reviewed the artillery of the corps and was ordered to prepare for another campaign. November 8th Captain Barnett resigned, and proceded to Atlanta with Lieutenant Coe. November 10th he left for Illinois, accompanied as far as Nashville by Quartermaster Brown. Lieutenant Coe assumed command of the battery, and having only one commissioned officer, promoted Orderly Sergeant Ward to Junior 2nd Lieutenant, and wrote to Governor Yates for his commission.

36. *Sherman*, Vol. 2, p. 156–57.

Quartermaster Sergeant Brown here severed his connection with [the] battery, as he never returned to active duty in its ranks. He was always an active business manager, looking out at all times for the best interests of the battery, seeing that the men had plenty to eat and wear when they were to be had. He always had charge of the muster and pay-rolls, and they were generally without fault in diction or penmanship. Had not Thomas Betts taken his place Brown would have been more generally missed, but Betts who had been acting as Commissary Sergeant for some time was fully competent to fill his place.

Captain Barnett had been the life and ambition of Battery I. Barnett's battery was known throughout the Fourteenth Corps as one of its best batteries. He was a thorough disciplinarian, a terror to sluggards and slinks, appearing at times somewhat tyranical, but as an efficient drill-master and battery officer he had no superior in the army. He was always careful of his men in battle, to take the best positions for their safety and at the same time to make the guns do the greatest service. He always saw that the men were well clothed and fed, and generally made but few mistakes in his government. He was generous to a fault, and when he liked a man he never could do too much for him, though he had few favorites in the battery and those had to do their duty well or they felt his displeasure for their neglect.

November 13th the battery passed Allatoona Station, the 2nd Division began its work of tearing up the track and burning and bending the rails, making a thorough demolition of the railroad. The last train north was watched with a sort of sadness and satisfaction. Sadness to say "good-bye" to northern homes, satisfaction to feel that when heard from again the war would be that much nearer finished. On the 14th the division marched by "Old Kenesaw" for the last time, and on the 15th arrived at Atlanta, where the rest of the boys were found ready for the great "March to the Sea."

6

WITH SHERMAN
TO THE SEA

In which Battery I is with Sherman's forces on the famous "March to the Sea," from Atlanta to Savannah. Sherman's men had no real opposition, and fought no major battles; they lived off the country, and destroyed railroads and all else of military value (and sometimes property of nonmilitary value) in an area fifty to sixty miles wide between Atlanta and Savannah. On December 9, 1864, near Savannah, Lt. Alonzo Coe, commanding the Battery since Captain Barnett's resignation on November 8, was killed in a minor engagement. Lt. Judson Rich would command the Battery now until the war ended. In Savannah, the army rested, and prepared to march through the Carolinas.

THE FOLLOWING is taken from Sherman's *Memoirs.*[1]

On the 12th of November the railroad and telegraph communications with the rear were broken, and the army stood detached from all friends, dependent on its own resources and supplies. No time was to be lost; all the detachments were ordered to march rapidly for Atlanta, breaking up the railroad on route, and generally to so damage the country as to make it untenable to the enemy. By the 14th all the troops had arrived at or near Atlanta, and were according to orders, grouped into two wings, the right and left, commanded respectively by Major-Generals O. O. Howard and H. W. Slocum, both comparatively young men, but educated and experienced officers, fully competent to their command.

1. *Ibid.*, pp. 171–72.

The right wing was composed of the Fifteenth Corps, Major-General P. J. Osterhaus commanding, and the Seventeenth Corps, Major-General Frank P. Blair commanding.

The left wing was composed of the Fourteenth Corps, Major-General Jefferson C. Davis commanding, and the Twentieth Corps, Brigadier-General A. S. Williams commanding . . .

. . . .

The Fourteenth Corps had three divisions, commanded by Brigadier-Generals W. P. Carlin, James D. Morgan, and A. Baird . . .

. . . .

The cavalry division was held separate, subject to my own orders. It was commanded by Brigadier-General Judson Kilpatrick, and was composed of two brigades, commanded by Colonels Eli H. Murray, of Kentucky, and Smith D. Atkins, of Illinois.

The strength of the army, as officially reported, is given in the following tables [not included], and shows an aggregate of fifty-five thousand three hundred and twenty nine infantry, five thousand and sixty-three cavalry, and eighteen hundred and twelve artillery—in all, sixty-two thousand two hundred and four officers and men.

Battery I marched "from Atlanta to the Sea" with the 2nd Division commanded by James D. Morgan,[2] and along with it marched "our old brigade," though the genial, manly face of Dan. McCook was sadly missed, riding at its head. Previous to the start from Atlanta the battery had been reduced to a four-gun battery, with eight horses to each gun and caison; and all superfluous baggage was turned over to the quartermaster of the army. There were only two commissioned officers with the battery, Lieutenant Coe, commanding, and Lieutenant Judson Rich. George T. Ward had been appointed lieutenant, but had not received his commission. Rugus S. Stolp had been promoted to Orderly Sergeant *vice* Ward promoted. The following extract is taken from an article written for the *Century Magazine* by Daniel Oakey.[3]

2. As already noted, Battery I had been in the Artillery Brigade of the 14th Corps since July, 1864. On November 18, 1864, the batteries in the Artillery Brigade were distributed, one to each division, and one to constitute Corps Artillery Reserve. Battery I was assigned to the 2nd Division of Brigadier General James D. Morgan, but was never a part of

Before the middle of November, 1864, the inhabitants of Atlanta, by Sherman's orders, had left the place. Serious preparations were making for the march to the sea. Nothing was to be left for the use or advantage of the enemy. The sick were sent back to Chattanooga and Nashville along with every pound of baggage that could be dispensed with. The army was reduced, one might say, to its fighting weight, no men being retained who was not capable of a long march. Our communications were then abandoned by destroying the railroad and telegraph. There was something intensely exciting in this perfect isolation.

The engineers had peremptory orders to avoid any injury to dwellings, but to apply gunpowder and the torch to public buildings, machine-shops, depots, and arsenals. Sixty thousand of us witnessed the destruction of Atlanta, while our post band and that of the 33d Massachusetts played martial airs and operatic selections. It was a night never to be forgotten. Our regular routine was a mere form, and there could be no "taps" amid the brilliant blare and excitement.

The throwing away of superfluous conveniencies began at daybreak. The old campaigner knows what to carry and what to throw away. Each group of messmates decided which hatchet, stew-pan, or coffee-pot should be taken. The single wagon allowed to a battalion carried scarcely more than a gripsack and blanket, and a bit of shelter tent about the size of a large towel for each officer, and only such other material as was necessary for regimental business. Transportation was reduced to a minimum, and fast marching was to be the order of the day. Wagons to carry the necessary ammunition in the contingency of a battle, and a few days' rations in case of absolute need, composed the train of each army corps, and with one wagon and one ambulance for each regiment made a very respectable "impedimenta," averaging about eight hundred wagons to a corps.

We copy from Sherman's *Memoirs* because the time and scene is so well described in the following extracts.[4]

the division.—See *O. R.*, Series I, Vol. 44, p. 489.

3. This quotation appears in an article written by Daniel Oakey titled "Marching Through Georgia and the Carolinas" in *B. & L.*, Vol. 4, p. 672.

4. *Sherman*, Vol. 2, pp. 178–84.

BEHIND THE GUNS

About 7 A.M. of November 16th we rode out of Atlanta by the Decatur road, filled by marching troops and wagons of the Fourteenth Corps; and reaching the hill, just outside of the old rebel works, we naturally pause to look back upon the scenes of our past battles . . . Behind us lay Atlanta, smouldering and in ruins, the black smoke raising high in air, and hanging like a pall over the ruined city. Away off in the distance, on the McDonough road, was the rear of Howard's column, the gun-barrels glistening in the sun, the white-topped wagons stretching away to the south; and right before us the Fourteenth Corps, marching steadily and rapidly, with a cheery look and swinging pace, that made light of the thousand miles that lay between us and Richmond. Some band, by accident, struck up the anthem of "John Brown's soul goes marching on"; the men caught up the strain, and never before or since have I heard the chorus of "Glory, glory, Hallelujah!" done with more spirit, or in better harmony of time and place.

Then we turned our horses heads to the east; Atlanta was soon lost behind the screen of trees, and became a thing of the past . . . The day was extremely beautiful, clear sunlight, with bracing air, and an unusual feeling of exhilaration seemed to pervade all minds—a feeling of something to come, vague and undefined, still full of venture and intense interest. Even the common soldiers caught the inspiration, and many a group called out to me as I worked my way past them, "Uncle Billy, I guess Grant is waiting for us at Richmond!

. . . .

The first night out we camped by the roadside near Lithonia. Stone Mountain, a mass of granite, was in plain view, cut out in clear outline against the blue sky, the whole horizon was lurid with the bonfires of railties, and groups of men all night were carrying the heated rails to the nearest trees, and bending them around the trunks . . . The next day we passed through the handsome town of Covington, the soldiers closing up their ranks, the color bearers unfurling their flags, and the bands striking up patriotic airs. The white people came out of their houses to behold the sight, spite of their deep hatred of the invaders, and the negroes were simply frantic with joy.

. . . .

From Covington the Fourteenth Corps (Davis's), with which I was traveling, turned to the right for Milledgeville, via

Shady Dale. . . . We found abundance of corn molasses, meal, bacon, and sweet potatoes. We also took a good many cows and oxen, and a large number of mules. In all these the country was quite rich, never before having been visited by a hostile army; the recent crop had been excellent, had been just gathered and laid by for winter. As a rule, we destroyed none, but kept our wagons full, and fed our teams bountifully.

.   .   .   .

Habitually each corps followed some main road, and the foragers, being kept out on the exposed flank, served all the military use of flankers. The main columns gathered, by the roads traveled, much forage and food, chiefly meat, corn, and sweet potatoes, and it was the duty of each division and brigade quartermaster to fill his wagons as fast as the contents were issued to the troops. The wagon-trains had the right to the road *always*, but each wagon was required to keep closed up, so as to leave no gaps in the column. If for any purpose any wagon or group of wagons dropped out of place, they had to wait for the rear. And this was always dreaded, for each brigade commander wanted his train up at camp as soon after reaching it with his men as possible . . . Habitually we started from camp, at the earliest break of dawn, and usually reached camp soon after noon. The marches varied from ten to fifteen miles a day, though sometimes on extreme flanks it was necessary to make as much as twenty, but the rate of travel was regulated by the wagons; and, considering the nature of the roads, fifteen miles per day was deemed the limit.

The battery camped near Tatonton [Eatonton] Factory on the 21st, the night being unusually cold and raw and a high wind blowing. From this place to Milledgeville was ten miles, and there was here an old fashioned railroad with wooden stringers on ties and a bar of strap iron for the wheels to run on, which made traveling dangerous, on account of these bars becoming loosened when they would roll up and run through the car floor. Near this place was the plantation of [Major] General Howell Cobb, of Georgia, one of the leading rebels of the South. Of course everything on that plantation was confiscated, and everything destroyed that would burn. Late in the evening of the 22nd of November the division arrived at Milledgeville after six days march of pleasure and plenty. Time hung not heavily on their hands, nor did the ghost of hunger haunt them in their dreams, but rather the nightmare of plentious engorgement. The boys laid down to rest at night, after a day's march, on beds of pine boughs with as much composure and comfort, as if they had been downy feather beds. The following is taken from the *History* of the 86th Illinois infantry.[5]

> There was a great caravan of negroes hanging on the rear of our column when it arrived at Milledgeville, like a sable cloud in the sky before a thunder storm or tornado. They thought it was freedom now or never, and would follow whether or no. It was really a ludicrous sight to see them trudging on after the army in promiscuous style and divers manners. Some in buggies of the most costly and glittering manufacture; some on horseback, the horses old and blind, and others on foot; all following up in right jolly mood, bound for the elysium of ease and freedom. Let those who choose to curse the negro curse him; but one thing is true, despite the unworthiness they bear on many minds, that they were the only friends on whom we could rely for the sacred truth in the sunny land of Dixie. What they said might be relied on, so far as they knew; and one thing more, they knew more and could tell more than most of the poor white population.

While at Milledgeville some of the boys witnessed the following scene in the State Capitol building: "Some of the officers (in the spirit of mischief) gathered together in the vacant hall of Representatives, elected a Speaker, and constituted themselves the Legislature of the State of Georgia! A proposition was made to repeal the ordinance of secession, which was well debated, and resulted in its repeal by a fair vote!"[6]

On the morning of the 24th the 2nd Division marched through Milledgeville, and arrived at Sandersville on the 26th, where it remained in camp till the 28th, waiting for the right wing to catch up

---

5. *86th Illinois*, pp. 80–81.
6. *Sherman*, Vol. 2, p. 190.   7. *Ibid.*, p. 191.
8. See Brigadier General James D Morgan's, "Report," *O. R.*, Series I, Vol. 44, p. 180: "While at Louisville six wagons, under charge of Lt. Coe, acting assistant Quartermaster, were attacked just outside of picket-line by Wheeler's cavalry, and four wagons captured, the remaining two

with the left. Sherman says: [7] "A brigade of rebel cavalry was deployed before the town, and was driven in and through it by our skirmishers line. I myself saw the rebel cavalry apply fire to stacks of fodder standing in the fields at Sandersville, and gave orders to burn some unoccupied dwellings close by."

The division left Sandersville about noon of the 28th, and arrived on the west bank of Rocky Comfort Creek that afternoon. The bridge over this stream having been burned the troops were obliged to wait till late in the evening before crossing could be affected into Louisville, where they went into camp about a mile east of the village.

On the 29th the enemy's cavalry made a demonstration on our lines, when a regiment of infantry was ordered to the front, and there threw up a line of baricades for a protection. A constant fire was kept upon the rebels, and they fell back in confusion across a large cornfield, in the edge of which they formed their line and threw up a line of breastworks which they held till late in the afternoon, when the infantry charged them, driving them, and taking possession of their baricades, and then followed them for over a mile.[8]

Every morning a detail of men, in command of a sergeant went out foraging for the battery, and they most always came into camp with an unlimited supply of hams, chickens, and sweet potatoes, for the men, and plenty of forage for the horses. Sergeant Ed. Smith was one of the most persistent foragers in the battery; he rarely came into camp without his team being well loaded down with good things. He did not hesitate on one occasion, when the battery was in front of Savannah, and meat was getting scarce in camp, to kill a good fat mule he accidentally found, dressed it, brought it to the battery, and divided it amongst the men. They, not knowing that it was mule meat, relished it and thought it was the best of beef. Many good horses and mules were brought in for the battery use; among

escaping within the lines, followed by the enemy. Captain Dunphy, with Company [G], Tenth Michigan Infantry, waited coolly their approach; when within close range fired, killing 1 lieutenant, 2 privates, and wounding 2 (1 mortally); promptly charging, recaptured the four wagons . . . The enemy did not wait for a close approach to deployed infantry, but made a rapid retreat."

the best was a fine bay team of coach horses, which had been captured on a flat boat that was just putting off to cross the Savannah River. They were used as a wheel team, and made a powerful span for that place. An amusing event took place in connection with that team. As has been told, wagons had the right of way on the roads on account of the importance of their loads. One day the battery was moving along when it was met by a number of wagons, leading which was a fine six-mule team, driven by a sturdy "mule whacker," who would not give the road to the battery. Lieutenant Coe came to the front and ordered the fellow to give way, but the fellow with an oath told him to get out of the road with his "old battery"; Coe ordered the drivers to hitch onto his old wagon and pull him out of the way. "All right," says the man, "two can work that game." With an oath or two and a crack of his long whip he yelled "Ge-lang, what do I feed yer for," the gun and the wagon locked wheels and came to a standstill, both mules and horses tugging at their best and no move could be made by either. Finally Lieutenant Coe having great faith in the coach horses, shouted to the driver, "Let them have the whip!" The postillion struck both horses a savage blow and yelled at the same time. There was a crash and a bursting of chains and harness. The team had freed itself from the gun. With another crack of his whip and an oath the "mule whacker" shouted, "Ge-lang!" and over went the gun bottom side up, while the driver looking back said, "Pick up yer d——d old gun, and don't try to stop a gentleman on the road again."

The *History* of the 86th Illinois gives the following:[9]

> On the first of December, the division moved from Louisville in the direction of Millen, and crossing on its route, Big, Dry, and Spring Creeks, camped a short distance to the east of the latter. It had the corps train in charge, while the other two divisions moved on the right and left to protect it.
>
> The next day a deflection was made in the line of march of our division, caused by the change of direction of the 20th Corps, its course being turned northwards, crossing Buckhead and Rocky Creeks, on pontoons laid for that purpose, and camping on the night of the 3rd at Lumpkin's on the railroad. On the next day Carlin's and Morgan's divisions, with the

9. *86th Illinois*, p. 84.

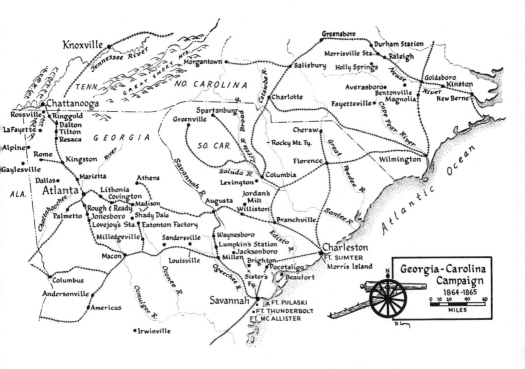

Map legend:

Georgia-Carolina
Campaign
1864-1865
0 10 20 40 60
MILES

three corps trains, after destroying three miles of railroad, moved in the direction of Jacksonboro, and camped thirteen miles beyond Lumpkin's Station. On this same day, Baird and Kilpatrick, after some fighting with Wheeler's cavalry, drove the enemy from Waynesboro and across Brier creek. The march was continued on the morning of the 5th, passing through Jacksonboro into the northeastern edge of Effingham County, thence down the Savannah River, arriving in the vicinity of the city of Savannah on the 11th of December.

On the afternoon of the 9th of December, when the division was within fifteen miles of Savannah, their line of march was disputed by a rebel battery planted at the crossing of two roads, just at the end of a causeway through a swamp. Lieutenant Coe ordered one section of the battery, under the command of Lieutenant Ward, to the front, which was supported by the 86th and 125th Illinois infantry. The position was a very much exposed one, being on a narrow road with a dense swampy growth on both sides. The horses and men were kept to the side of the way as much as possible, but the rebel battery had a plain sweep with nothing to obstruct the view. Sergeant Ed. Smith opened with his gun, and after getting the range dismounted one of the rebel guns and blew up a caison. Lieutenant Coe, who considered himself a good gunner, thought he would try his skill at the gun, but before he stepped to position a rebel shell hit him just as the sword belt, cutting it in three pieces, and passed through the body. With the cry, "My god, I'm shot!" he dropped dead.[10] Lieutenant Ward sent word back to Lieutenant Rich, who was with the other section, about a half mile in the road, that Lieutenant Coe had been killed, and Rich immediately assumed command of the battery.

Two horses were killed and one wounded in the same position. The two Regiments were ordered to deploy a heavy skirmish line and advance, but night came on and no action took place and in the morning the works were evacuated. What there was left of the rebel battery was captured the next day, having, in the darkness, taken the wrong road which led them into the Union lines. There was no other casualties besides the death of Lieutenant Coe at this time. He was in command of the battery since Captain Barnett resigned, and was well liked by the men. That night a rude coffin was prepared, and, with the brigade band in the lead, the coffin draped with "Old Glory," placed on a caison, the battery-men following in sad procession each man bearing a pine torch, the body was borne to the grave which had been dug between two large pine trees upon the plantation of Dr. Kyler, and there buried with the usual military ceremonies. A head-board was placed at the head of the grave, and a fence of rails was built around it. His body was subsequently removed by his widow and taken to his native state, New York, and entered in the family burying ground.

On the 10th the command moved to within three miles of Savannah, taking a position in the line of investment on the left, not far from the river. The battery camped in a thick pine woods to the left of one of the principal roads leading into Savannah, not far from a gravel pit, which became a great resort for "chuck luck" players.

10. "At Doctor Cuyler's Plantation, about fourteen miles and a half from Savannah, my advance came within range and fire of a rebel battery. Two regiments of the Third Brigade were at once deployed as skirmishers on the right and left of the road, and one piece of the battery ordered forward. This piece was soon in position and opened fire, which was spiritedly answered by some well-directed shots. Lieutenant Coe, commanding battery, was struck by a shell and instantly killed; a brave, good

The boys had received their pay just before starting on the "March to the Sea," and had not had any chance to spend it, so there was plenty of funds for gambling. The commanding officer did not like the idea of the boys gambling, so ordered the guards to arrest any caught in the act of running a "chuck luck" table. To protect themselves they took possession of this gravel pit and posted pickets to give the alarm when the guards approached. Many was the scare and flight from that pit of gambling, and many the dollar that changed hands without being won or lost when a rush came to escape arrest.

The rebels had a line of breastworks surrounding Savannah, and at all roads they had heavy guns of English make bearing on the causeways through the swamps or lowlands. On the 20th the left section of the battery was moved forward into bastions built on the road, by the 17th New York Zouaves, within four hundred yards of the rebel works.[11] During the night the "Johnies" kept up a continual fire from the large siege guns, wounding several of the New York Zouaves. The next morning, at daylight, it was discovered that a shell from one of those guns had cut down a tree, which had fallen in front of one of the guns of the left section, obstructing the view, whereupon a detail was made to remove it. Sergeant Murphy suggested that a prolonge [12] be thrown across the road to the tree and made fast to it, and then the men could haul it out of the way. Alonzo Kelly, a cannoneer, volunteered to make the rope fast, though it would be a dangerous undertaking. He waved his hands to his comrades, and sprang over the bastion, making the prolonge fast to the tree, the boys, under cover of the thick brush on the side of the road, pulled it out of the way. Just as they were ready to open on the rebel works someone remarked that the rebel line was suspiciously silent, and that there might be a chance that the works were empty. Sergeant Murphy and Alonzo Kelly cautiously made their way to

officer. By order subsequently received from corps commander the First and Third Brigades were placed in position. During the night the works in our front were abandoned."—Brigadier James. D. Morgan, "Report," *O. R.*, Series I, Vol. 44, p. 181. 11. See *O. R.*, Series 1, Vol. 44, p. 769. 12. A prolonge was a heavy rope which could be used to shift a light field piece a short distance, when it seemed unnecessary or unwise to hitch up the horses; it was kept coiled on the trail of the gun.

their fortifications and peeked in through one of the embrasures. There they saw two darkies, one asleep and the other sitting on an empty cracker-box. Upon being questioned as to what had become of the rebels, they replied that they had gone sometime in the night, but had left a few torpedoes planted on the railroad to our left.

A little earlier than this event the "White Star" division of the 20th Corps, discovering that the rebel lines were evacuated, marched into the city of Savannah just as the rear of Hardee's division was crossing the river on a pontoon bridge. The Mayor of the city surrendered to General Geary, who immediately took possession and established a provost guard for its protection and government. The 2nd Division camped in the suburbs, on the west side, and the battery had its camp beside a canal. The following is taken from the *History* of the 86th Illinois.[13]

> Up the Savannah River from the city of Savannah, and bordering on it, upon either bank, were large and flourishing rice plantations, cultivated by great numbers of negroes of every hue of the skin and brogue of the tongue; some of them direct from Liberia, some from New Guinea; and others from the swamps of Florida . . .
>
> .   .   .   .
>
> Great ricks of this precious produce, in every way resembling oats, were stacked on each plantation, and from ten to twenty thousand bushels in a single stack-yard. Our army made use of it in various ways, much of it being threshed and hulled, and then used by the soldiers, but a greater part fed to mules.

Sherman in his *Memoirs* says:[14]

> At that interview, Mr. Browne who was a shrewd, clever Yankee, told me that a vessel was on the point of starting for Old Point Comfort, and, if she had good weather off Cape Hatteras, would reach Fortress Monroe by Christmas-day, and he suggested that I might make it the occasion of sending a welcome Christmas gift to the President, Mr. Lincoln, who peculiarly enjoyed such pleasantry. I accordingly sat down and wrote on a slip of paper, to be left at the telegraph-office at Fortress Monroe for transmission, the following:

13. *86th Illinois*, p. 88.   14. *Sherman*, Vol. 2, pp. 231–32.

Savannah, Georgia, December 22nd, 1864.

To His Excellency President Lincoln, Washington, D.C.:
I beg to present you as a Christmas-gift the city of Savannah, with one hundred and fifty heavy guns and plenty of ammunition, also about twenty five thousand bales of cotton.

W. T. Sherman, Major-General.

This message actually reached him on Christmas-eve, was extensively published in the newspapers, and made many a household unusually happy on that festive day; and it was the answer to this dispatch that Mr. Lincoln wrote me the letter of December 28th.

In Sherman's raid to the sea the army marched over three hundred miles directly through the heart of Georgia, subsisting on the country where it was possible. No less than twelve thousand negroes left the plantations of their old masters and followed in the wake of Sherman's army, never to go back to slavery again.

The campaign "from Atlanta to the Sea" through Georgia, the largest state of the slaveholding confederacy, was practically unobstructed by the rebels. [Major General Joseph] Wheeler's cavalry would at times make a stand behind an entrenchment, and contest the advance of Sherman's forces, when the advance guard would have a little brush with them, soon scattering them, but they made no impression on the main army in the forward march to the coast in the way of staying its progress.

"The city of Savannah," as Sherman describes it,[15] "was an old place, and usually accounted a handsome one. Its houses were of brick or frame . . . its streets perfectly regular, crossing each other at right angles; and at many of the intersections were small inclosures in the nature of parks. These streets and parks were lined with the handsomest shadetrees of which I have knowledge, *viz.*, the willow-leaf live oak, evergreens of exquisite beauty; and these certainly entitled Savannah to its reputation as a handsome town more than the houses, which, though comfortable, would hardly make a display on Fifth Avenue or the Boulevard Hausemann of Paris. The city was built on a plateau of sand about forty feet above

15. *Ibid.*, pp. 230–31.

the level of the sea, abutting against the river, leaving room along its margin for a street of stores and warehouses. The custom-house, court-house, post-office, etc., were on the plateau above. In rear of Savannah was a large park, with a fountain, and between it and the court-house was a handsome monument, erected to the memory of Count Pulaski, who fell in 1779 in the assault made on the city at the time it was held by the English during the Revolutionary War. Outside of Savannah there was very little to interest a stranger, except the cemetery of Bonaventura, and the ride along the Wilmington Channel by way of Thunderbolt, where might be seen some groves of the majestic live-oak trees covered with gray and funereal moss, which were truly sublime in grandeur, but gloomy after a few day's camping under them."

"Savannah is located in a low, level country, surrounded by almost impassable swamps of a very unhealthy nature. It has a canal running into it from the Ogeechee, and three railroads radiating from it; and from its beautiful shade trees, it is appropriately called the 'Forest City.' " [16]

One incident occurred during the battery's march to the sea, which might be noted as showing the horrors of war. One morning Sergeant Ed. Smith started out before dawn at the head of a foraging party to collect supplies for the battery. He had a guard of about fifteen men armed with carbines, detailed for the purpose. Smith deployed his men along the road in advance of the wagons, and they were ordered to procede very cautiously along, looking constantly for "bush-whackers." Soon after starting, while it was yet dark, there was a squad of Union cavalry came up in the rear. The officer in charge hailed Smith, and asked him if he would move on faster. Smith replied, "No"; he would not go off of a walk until daylight. The officer then asked permission to pass the train, which request was freely granted. About daylight, as the wagons were moving along, the sharp crack of the cavalry carbine was heard about a half-mile ahead, showing that there was trouble. Smith at once ordered his men to close up, and go forward at a lively pace. After riding rapidly for a distance they came to an opening in the

16. This paragraph appears on page 89 of *86th Illinois*.

timber, in front of a fine house. On the greensward in the front yard there lay the dead bodies of the cavalrymen, which had so lately passed the train on the road, full of life and ambition. On one of the dead bodies was pinned a note on which was written, "Death to Sherman's foragers." Sergeant Smith immediately sent word back to General Jeff. C. Davis, commanding the 14th corps, who was soon on the ground. Upon his arrival he took a rapid survey of the sad spectacle, and in his indignation he rode up to the house, and in forcible terms ordered the inmates out, and then told his men to apply the torch, which soon rendered the beautiful home into a pile of ashes. Smith found plenty of provisions and forage in the barn and out-houses from which he loaded all of his wagons, then setting fire to the buildings, he started for the battery.

General Davis rightly conjectured that the rebels had used the house as an ambuscade, and that it was a clear case of murder by Southern "bush-whackers"; as they escaped he decided to deal out rightous punishment upon their sympathizers. It was war, cruel war, and women and children had to suffer as well as those who were bearing arms in the field.

Several of the Union foragers were killed while the army was moving through South Carolina, by the "Guerillas," in the same way. General Sherman sent word to the rebel general that for every Union soldier killed in that way, he would have shot—man for man—a rebel officer or an enlisted man, who had been taken prisoner. After that declaration none of the foragers were murdered.

At Savannah the army was weeded of all invalids or men unable to stand hard marching in an inclement season. The city hospital building was occupied for all its capacity, then other buildings and hotels were used for hospitals. A number of men from the battery were sent to the hospital, who never saw their comrades again for years, and some for life. Among those that left was Bugler Putney, who having contracted sore eyes and a hernia, while on the "March to the Sea" was obliged to enter the hospital for treatment. He had never left the ranks of the battery up to this time, being always ready to blow the calls in field or camp, and was considered by the boys as

133

one of the best buglers in the corps. For a time while in the hospital his eyes improved, but on his return home they became worse, and for nearly two years after his return they demanded constant treatment. Marshal Peterson took the place as bugler during the march through the Carolinas to Washington.

One by one the officers and men were leaving the ranks of the battery for home and hospital, though Battery I never suffered in battle as some did. The following is taken from the *History* of the 86th Illinois infantry.[17]

Sherman had pushed from the mountain districts of the north to the level lowlands of the south, no army having ever met with more signal success than his. No difficulties had been more successfully overcome, in any time or age, than by his exultant army. With determined zeal and firm tread it marched from one victory to another.

If it failed in driving the enemy at one or two or three trials, it was still fearless and determined. And he was a brave and mighty man who led this army through so many perils to lasting fame and achievements. It had been on an active campaign for eight long months, digging in the dirt and marching like the wind.

17. *Ibid.*, p. 91.

7

THE END OF

THE WAR:

AFTERMATH

None of the three men who compiled this history of Battery I were present with the Battery when it marched out of Savannah into the Carolinas. The Battery participated in the entire campaign, and was in the vicinity of Raleigh, North Carolina, when Johnston surrendered to Sherman. The chapter which ends their work and which covers the period January 1, 1864–June 14, 1864, is almost entirely composed of long quotations —not always acknowledged—from such participants as Generals Slocum and Sherman, and from regimental histories. Rather than weary the reader with a long series of quotations, it seems best to publish the itinerary of the Battery as it appears on the monthly returns, adding Lieutenant Judson Rich's "Report of operations January 20–March 23, 1865" (O. R., Series I, Vol. 47, Part 1, pp. 577–78) and closing with the last few pages written by our "Brave Bugler Putney."

January, 1865

1 In camp near Savannah, Ga. Moved a short distance to better camping ground & remained until 20th.

20 Then moved out on Louisville Road 9 miles, went into camp, and remained until 25th.

25	Then marched toward Sister's Ferry, made 15 miles, roads bad.
26	Marched through Springfield, Ga. distance unknown; roads worse.
27	Marched about 6 miles & camped—roads "worst."
28	Marched about 5 miles & came to camp on the bank of Savannah River near Sister's ferry.
31	Still in camp on the 31st.
February 1, 1865	In camp near Sister's Ferry, Ga., Laying in camp until Feb. 5th.
5	Then moved across Savannah River and camped near Brown's Ferry until 7th.
7	Then moved near river and relieved Reserve Arty in position, moved on the 8th.
8	About 8 miles & camped near Brighton, S.C.
9–12	Marching in northerly direction, crossed the S.C. R.R. near Williston.
13	Marched and camped near Jordan's Mills.
14 & 15	Marching.
16	Passed through Lexington and camped near Columbia, S.C.
17	Passed Eschula River & camped on Broad River, guns in position.
18	In camp.
19	Crossed the River. Marched about 4 miles. Camped for night. Guns in position.
20	Marched & camped near Little River.
21	Crossed River.
22	Marched & crossed R.R. near Youngstown.
23	Marched & camped near Catawba River. Heavy rains at night.
24	Crossed River & camped about 3 miles from River, Roads very bad & heavy rains continue. Still in camp on

28	Rain still continue 28th marched at 11 o'clock A.M. Made about 4 miles and camped for night.

March, 1865.

1	Marching (one day's march from Rock Mount Ferry) S.C.
2, 3 & 4	Marched—Camped night of the 4th on the Great Pedee River.
5 & 6	In camp.
7	Marched at 2 P.M. crossing the River.
8, 9, 10 & 11	Marching
12	In camp near Fayetteville, N.C. Marched at 7 A.M. passing through town crossing Cape Fear River.
13	Marched about 2 miles on the Raleigh Road and camped for the day.
14	In camp.
15, 16, 17 & 18	Marching on Goldsboro Road.
19	Marched. Found the enemy in force. Went into position and fired 217 rounds. Lay on the line until the 22nd. Enemy gone from our front. Marched.
23	Arrived at Goldsboro, N.C. went into camp.
25	Received an order relieving the battery from duty with the 2nd Div. 14th A.C. By order of Charles Houghtaling, Maj. & Chief of Arty., 14th A.C.
31	Still in camp near Goldsboro, N.C.

Report of Lieut. Judson Rich, Battery I, Second Illinois Light Artillery, of operations January 20–March 23.

Sir: I have the honor to make the following report of the part taken in the recent campaign from Savannah, Ga., to Goldsborough, N.C., by Battery I, Second Illinois Light Artillery:

January 20, 1865, at 8 A.M., I moved from Camp near Savannah, Ga., marching on the Louisville, Ga., road, attached to the Second Division, Fourteenth Army Corps; roads bad and weather rainy; made about nine miles; went into camp; lay until 25th, at 7 A.M.; marching each day until 28th; at night went into camp on the bank of Savannah River near Sister's Ferry, Ga.; in camp until February 5, 1865, then moved across the river on pontoon bridge to the South Carolina side; went into camp. 6th, in camp all day; drew and issued clothing to the men. 7th, moved near the bank of the river and went into position, relieving the reserve battery of Fourteenth Army Corps. 8th, marched at 7 A.M., marching each day until night of the 17th; went into camp on Broad River with guns in position, remaining until the 19th; at 7 A.M. moved across the river about four miles and camped with the guns in position. 20th, marches continued, marching each day. 24th, crossed the Catawba River near Rocky Mount Ferry; camped and lay in camp until 28th. At 11 A.M. marched, roads very bad, marching each day until March 4. At night went into camp near Great Pedee River; lay in camp until 7th. At 2 P.M. moved across the river and went into position on the left bank, covering the pontoon bridge and landing on the opposite bank until the bridge was taken up. 8th, at 6 A.M. marched on the Fayetteville road and continued from Fayetteville. 12th, in camp all day; marched at dark, passing through Fayetteville and crossing Cape Fear River. 13th, marched at 7 A.M.; made about two miles and camped on the Raleigh road; lay in camp until 15th. At 9 A.M. marched on the Goldsborough road. 16th, at 8.30 A.M. marched; found the enemy in front; battery did not get a position. Marched on 17th and 18th. 19th, marched about four miles and found the enemy in force; the enemy made an attack; we went into position and fired 217 rounds; the enemy was repulsed. 20th and 21st, on the line in position behind works. 22d, enemy gone from our front; marched to near Neuse River and camped for the night. 23d marched, crossing the river, passing through Goldsborough, and went into camp about two miles from the city.

Very respectfully, your obedient servant,

Judson Rich

April, 1865

1–10	In camp in Goldsboro, N.C.
10	Marched passing through Raleigh, N.C. arrived at Avers Ferry on Cape Fear River. In camp there until
21	Marched to Holly Springs, In camp there until
29	Marched to Morrisville Station.

30	In camp at Morrisville, N.C.

May, 1865

1	Marched from Morrisville Station near Raleigh, N.C. for Richmond, Va. Arrived on the 7th.
7	At Five Mile Creek and went into camp, 5 miles from Richmond, Va.
11	Marched, passing through the city of Richmond and marching on the Washington, D.C. Road.
19	Arrived near Alexandria, Va. and went in camp.
24	Marched through Washington City in Review.
25	Marched across the river to make camp near Fort Bunkerhill.
31	Still in camp.

On the 20th of May the army arrived at Alexandria, and went into camp to wait for the Grand Review. At this place Lieutenant McDonald and Warner Dibirt rejoined the battery, after being confined in rebel prisons since their capture near Big Shanty, Ga. They were very thin and pale, so much so, that the boys could hardly recognize them. McDonald has written up his experience while a prisoner of war, which will be given at the close of this chapter.

Upon their arrival at Washington the battery took part in the grand review of the whole army by President Johnson, General Grant, and others. Sherman's boys presented a rather dilapidated condition in comparison with the Eastern troops, but their long and rapid strides which they took in marching by the reviewing stand, showed they were men that were used to long marches, and they received quite an ovation. They marched by the way of the White House, Capitol, and Pennsylvania Avenue, and returned to their former camp in Alexandria.

Sergeant Murphy returned to the battery at this camp from Nashville, Tenn., and was detailed by General Davis as Commissary Sergeant of all the batteries belonging to the Fourteenth Corps.

May 25th the battery left camp at Alexandria, and passed through Washington, and went into camp about three miles from the city. May 29th news of the surrender of Kirby Smith was received, which finished up the Confederacy. May 30th Captain Rich turned over all the equipments of the battery to

139

the ordinance department, and now the boys were ready to go to that "prairie state" they had so longed to see, and be mustered out. The men had a very enjoyable time taking in Washington, viewing all the sights and curiosities of the place while lying in camp so near the city, but all were anxious to go home to their loved ones. June 1st the boys took the cars en route via Baltimore and Ohio R.R., through Indiana to Springfield, Ill., where they arrived on the 7th and went into the barracks at Camp Butler. Here the men waited till the final muster-out and pay-rolls were completed. On the 11th Sergeant Murphy joined the battery, having been left behind at Washington.

June 14th the men of the battery were mustered out of the service of Uncle Sam, each was given his discharge papers and paid off, and all were now citizens of the State of Illinois, possessing the privilege of depositing a ballot, which had been denied them while in the army. Those who had in such close companionship through so many battles, bivouacked on many a field and camp, shared the same mess and drank from the same canteen, now bid good-bye to each other and scatter to their several homes, there to meet the loved ones at the family fireside, from whom they have been separated through the long agonizing years of a bloody, fratricidal war.

None of the original officers were at the muster-out. The roster of the commissioned officers at the close of the war was as follows: Captain, Judson Rich; Sr. 1st Lieutenant, George T. Ward; Sr. 2nd Lieutenant, Chas. McDonald.

Battery I was in the service three years, eight months and sixteen days. It would be impossible to give the exact number of miles it marched during that time. It was only absent from the field of active operations when veteranizing and recruiting, previous to the Atlanta campaign. In the course of its travels it visited ten of the Southern states, which took part in the Rebellion. Florida, Louisiana, and Texas were the only rebel states that did not get a taste of its mettle and metal. About fifty men of the original number or roster returned with the battery, though its ranks were often recruited.

In conclusion we quote from the finale of Carlton's *Boys of '61:* [1]

---

[1]. Charles Carleton Coffin. *The Boys of '61; or, Four Years of Fighting* (Boston: Estes and Lauriat, 1884), p. 558.

How lavish the expenditure of blood! How generous the outpouring of the wine of life by the heroic dead!

> *Son of peace, nor battle's roar,*
> *Ne'er shall break their slumbers more;*
> *Death shall keep his solemn trust,*
> *"Earth to earth, and dust to dust."*

Dead, yet living. Their patriotism, sacrifice, endurance, patience, faith, and hope can never die. Loved and lamented, but immortal. Paeons for the living, dirges for the dead. Their work is done, nor for an hour, a day, a year, but for all time; not for fame or ambition, but for the poor, the degraded, the oppressed of all lands, for civilization and Christianity for the welfare of the human race through time and Eternity!

APPENDICES

INDEX

APPENDIX 1

LIFE IN REBEL PRISONS

The following is a description of the capture and life in rebel prisons, given to Sergeant Murphy by Lieutenant Charles McDonald in which he says:

Dear Comrade.—

I promised you when I wrote again to give you a description of how, when, and where, I became a prisoner of war. You probably recollect the field in which the battery camped on Saturday eve near Big Shanty, Ga., there being a field of ripe barley adjoining, from which the postillions cut grain for their horses.

Bright and early Sabbath morning, May 7th, 1864, Lieutenant Coe, believing that there must be corn found between the lines at the front, went to division headquarters and procured passes for Lieutenant McDonald and four men, which gave permission to go outside the lines for the purpose of procuring forage for the battery. General Davis saw me before I started and ordered me, on my return, to report how the ground lay in front, as there was a prospect of a fight soon. It was very lucky for Bugler Putney that his horse needed shoeing, as he was very anxious to go with the party. Had he gone that would have been the last of Putney.

Well, with Warner Dibirt riding close behind, I spurred my horse to the front, where at the picket line I found Dick Knott, who at one time was a detailed man to the battery. He halted me, and, after examining my papers, told me to keep a sharp lookout for a squad of our cavalry, who he said had just gone out on the road and were probably about half a mile ahead. Poor fellows! I made their acquaintance that afternoon in the Marietta Jail. We

*did not go far. I was well satisfied that our movement was a
risky one. We soon turned back towards camp, and had not riden
far before we rode right into the ranks of a company of mounted
infantry belonging to the 45th Alabama. They had captured our
cavalry videttes, and were everyone of them dressed in the U.S.
uniform.*

*We were made to dismount immediately, and then the rebels
took all they could find about our persons, even to my good hat
which an aid of General Kelly grabbed from my head and placed
an old one in its stead. We were then taken to [Major] General
[William W.] Loring's headquarters, from thence to General
Wheeler's, where an adjutant of his, who was a countryman of
mine, tried to question me in regard to the position of our lines
and the condition of our army.*

*While at the headquarters of General Wheeler I was taken for
Frank Sherman, a cousin of General Sherman. From General
Wheeler's headquarters we were taken to Marietta jail, tramping
all the way with nothing to eat. The jail being full they put us
in the court-house where, it being Sunday, the citizens brought
their wives and sweethearts to see the "live Yankees."*

*The next morning we were taken from the court-house and put
in boxcars, and given two army bisquits, which were to supply
us for breakfast, dinner, and supper. We were all unloaded at
Atlanta where they marched us to a place called the "bull pen."
Here we saw an escaped prisoner from Andersonville, waiting
to be sent back. We were kept in the "pen" for three days, during
which time I was busy instructing Dibirt how to protect himself
from scurvy. On the morning of the fourth day we were taken
from the "pen" and Dibirt and I were separated, not to meet
again till near the close of the war. I arrived at Macon the same
day, but Dibirt was taken to Andersonville where he suffered all
that "hell" could give in the way of deprivation and torture.
After entering the prison at Macon the first man I saw to know
was old Captain Hescock, of Battery G 1st Missouri, the next
was Captain Conner, of the 125th Illinois, and a Lieutenant of
the same regiment, I have forgotten his name. Poor fellow, he lost
his life while there in prison. The Lieutenant was a man, but the
captain was a rascal.*

*I will here give you a sketch of how the Lieutenant was
killed. He and myself were quartered near a spring in a corner of
the stockade under a large pine tree. As the rebels had taken everything I had the Lieutenant shared his blanket with me. It rained*

*so often during the months of June and July, that it made us
very uncomfortable and consequently very unhappy; however, we
did not despair, and thought we saw the road to liberty by
crawling out under the stockade where a little stream of water
had its exit from the prison, which stream served to keep the
prison-camp healthy by carrying off the filth. By this exit we two
saw freedom, or thought we did, but alas! poor fellow, he met
his death instead. We had made our plans all complete, and only
waited for the first cloudy day or night to try and escape. We
drew lots to see who should go under the stockade first, and if
successful in getting away, we should make for Atlanta and then
try and get inside our lines, then in front of Atlanta. The lot fell
to the Lieutenant to go first, and the attempt was made during
a thunderstorm. I believe the rebel guards had been watching
us from the start, for the Lieutenant succeeded in getting
through, and I was about to follow, when I heard the report of
a gun, saw a blinding flash, heard the call of "corporal of the
guard," then I dodged back for safety. That was the last I ever
saw of my friend the Lieutenant. He lies buried in an unknown
grave somewhere near the Macon Fair-grounds. A few evenings
later another was shot to death near the same place in the same
vain attempt to escape.*

*While in Macon prison the Fourth of July came, and we had
a grand celebration. By eight o'clock in the forenoon 1,200
hungry and vermin-clad prisoners were gathered in groups, with
improvised glee-clubs singing patriotic songs, while others were
making speeches to enthusiastic audiences. I never saw such
patriotism displayed. Hungry men, ragged men, sick men, all
joined in the demonstration. While [we were] well under headway
in celebrating, the commanding officers at the head of about a
hundred guards, charged into our midst and taking some of the
prisoners placed them in close confinement in the town jail. Others
were chased up into corners where they were jabbed with
bayonets in a cruel manner, with the idea that they were doing a
glorious thing for the Southern Confederacy. Captain Gibbs, the
commandant, was censured and relieved of command, as he was
considered to be too lenient towards the prisoners.*

*Things went along in a hum-drum way till the 22nd of July,
when we distinctly heard the cannonading of the battle on the
left of Atlanta. There was a grand hurry-scurry to get us out of
Macon, as they thought that an attempt would be made to
liberate us by a cavalry raid.*

147

BEHIND THE GUNS

Our rations while in Macon consisted of one pint of cornmeal per day, a little salt once a week, three tablespoonsful of rice per week, six ounces of bacon per week, and once in a while a spoonful of brown peas.

After the fall of Atlanta orders came for six hundred prisoners to be moved. All wanted to be among the favored ones to leave. The same night six hundred more were ordered off, and I happened to be one of the second lot. We were crowded into old box cars, sixty to a car, with ten guards on top, with loaded muskets, ready to shoot the moment a hand should be exposed outside the car-door. It was a terrible place to stay in for sixty hours, no one even allowed to leave the cars to answer to the calls of nature. At Milledgeville, Ga. we were kept some hours on the side track, where I made another effort to escape. I got into the good graces of one of the guards, who allowed me to go for water for him, while the officers in charge were at dinner. A waiter at the hotel saw me go into a cornfield back of the hotel with the canteen in my hand, and he gave the alarm. I was taken back, but gave a reasonable excuse for stepping into the cornfield, so escaped being punished. After long delays coupled with bad treatment we were dumped out of the cars at Savannah, Ga. While in prison at Savannah we had a few weeks of fairly good rations, getting fresh meat three times a week, and about eight ounces of bacon, and our meal rations were larger and better. We also received rice, and were allowed to have tents in which we were allowed to build bunks from lumber furnished us. All this was due to an old Scotchman, the commissary, as no meaner man than Major Wayne, who had charge of the prisoners here, ever lived. The old Scotchman told me that he had spent forty thousand dollars of his own money rather than see the prisoners suffer and starve.

Tunneling was our main occupation while at Savannah. From my tent we ran a tunnel under the brick walls of the Marine Hospital grounds. We had about twenty feet dug when an old cow grazing along outside the wall broke into our tunnel. About ten of us got out, but in the hurry and confusion of the escape, instead of taking the swamp road to Fort McAllister, we took a street that led back into the city, where we ran into the city guards, and were taken to jail and kept on bread and water for a day or two, till [Major] General [Lafayette] McLaws paid us a visit, and consoled us by a threat of dire vengeance, if any farther attempts were made to escape. We were then sent back to the pen where we found another tunnel had been started, but it did not progress far before we had orders to move. At this time there had been organized societies called "The Council of Ten," in which each was bound by a strong oath to obey the orders of the Council. There were about three hundred members, which were divided into groups, and passwords and signs were given to all who joined. Captain Hescock and myself belonged to the same Council or group.

Plans had been laid that in our movement the train should be captured, and the guards should be taken prisoners, when all should make their way to our lines at Pocotaligo, S.C., taking our prisoners with us. On nearing Pocotaligo the train was side-tracked not far from a swamp for some hours, where after awhile a train ran along side with three-hundred South Carolina cadets on board. These were put on top of our cars, and the Major in command who was naturally a kind man, stepped in front of us and told us that all of our plans had been given away by one of our own men, that that man was even then in one of the passenger cars beside us in company with the rebel officers. Thus did our scheme, so secretly planned with such strong oath-binding end in a miserable failure, because one hungry, half starved renegade, who, for food and favor, gave away the secret of our plans. I expect that the villain was well rewarded, and is probably now a leading citizen of the State of South Carolina.

The train ran on to Charleston, S.C., where six hundred of us were put in the jail-yard, and kept there as hostages without shelter and with very little to eat. Here we were under the fire of the Morris Island batteries and the gunboat fleet, also the "Swamp Angel" threw its 100-pound shells over us. One of the nightly occupations was to watch the burning fuses to see if the shells were coming our way.

While here the Yellow Fever broke out, but the rebel guards were the first to suffer. Oh, it was an awful place! No shelter, and the September and October chilling winds blowing their bleak gales around the jail and work-house where the first six hundred were safely housed. Three hundred more were in the Roper Hospital when the Yellow Fever broke out among the guards. It was expected by the rebel authorities that the Fever would take off the "hated Yanks," but instead it decimated the ranks of the "Johnnies" themselves. General Hardee ordered all of the prisoners to be removed, as the Fever was taking more of *the guards than the prisoners. Dr. Todd, who was surgeon-in-chief at Charlston, had recommended to the Confederate officials that the most efficient way to dispose of the prisoners would be to put them in Charleston, and the Fever would do the rest. It is strange to say, but those that were strongest and the best fed, were the first to succumb to the dread disease. Those prisoners who received money from the north from relatives and friends, and thus were enabled to buy good things to eat, were the first to die with the fever.*

Again we were ordered to move, no one knew where. We had the same kind of conveyance, and had also plenty of chances to escape, and many took the opportunity to get away. We were hurried off to the interior of the State, where near Branchville we all thought our doom was sealed. With some others I tried to escape by sawing through the side of the car with table knives made into saws. At a place where the train stopped beside a large woodpile we crawled out and crept around behind the wood, and then made a rush for liberty, but the rebels soon put blood-hounds on our tracks and we were retaken. Poor Lieutenant Wilson was torn to pieces before my eyes by those terrible dog-fiends.

Finally we were safely landed in Columbia, the capitol of South Carolina, where we were kindly given the privilege of staying in the depot yard, during a heavy rain-storm, without shelter and nothing to eat for the space of two days. The prisoners were marched from this place across the Saluda River, and there turned into an old cotton field like a herd of cattle. In this field we were kept for five long months, though a part of the time I spent in the Insane Assylum grounds in the city, called Camp Sorghum, at which place I surely thought I should lay my bones. During my stay in Camp Sorghum I had the most exciting event transpire that ever happened while I was in the service of Uncle Sam.

December 8th, 1864, the weather was cold and the night was frosty. Every morning most of the prisoners went to a small stream that ran through the camp ground to bathe. There was a pack of blood-hounds kept here for hunting down runaways from prison, also to hunt up deserters from the military who guarded us. Of course the hounds and the keeper were intensely hated by the guards as well as the guarded. On the morning named the prisoners were, as usual, in the creek in great numbers. The hounds were being led around the camp to find

out whether any escapes had been made during the night. Some
one began to call the dogs, I with the rest, at the same time was
hurrying to make my toilet which from the scarcity of my
wardrobe you can plainly see would not take long to complete.
The hounds which were coupled together with locked couplings
came directly to me. I hurried them up among the "dugouts,"
and after getting them there was in a quandary to know what to
do with them, as all the rest of the boys seemed afraid to help
me. I called for a volunteer to hold them while I procured an
ax with which to kill the dogs. Just think of the situation. There
was the owner with a double-shot gun, the guards with loaded
muskets, all looking for a chance to get a crack at me, and I
holding the dogs for dire vengeance for the death of friend
Wilson. An old Floridian stepped to the front and made a little
speech that I shall never forget. Here is his speech: "Gentlemen,
I was in the Black Hawk War; I was in the Seminole War;
I was in the Mexican War; and by G——d I will hold the
hounds." At the finish of his harangue he grabbed the dogs
while I ran to Captain McKnight's tent for an ax, and in less
than a minute the dead dogs were in a hole, ten feet deep,
and covered up. In the meantime the owner was running around,
to and fro, having lost sight of his hounds, while all the eighteen-
hundred prisoners were running hither and thither, apparently
to help him, but in reality to cover me and my movements. When
he was informed what had become of his dogs, and saw what
was going in camp, he reported it to the officers who ordered
all of the cannon to be manned, and all of the guards were
called out, but I was thoroughly hidden by this time. The
prison was searched, the dead dogs were found and taken out
for burial, after which the owner came into camp and offered
five-hundred-dollars reward for the man who had killed his
hounds, but found no takers. The day wore on and the excitement died out, and I, you may rest assured, breathed more
freely. The next day everything was as calm as a Sabbath day.

In Camp Sorghum, having no shelter, our clothes rotted off
our bodies. My wardrobe, at this time, consisted of a pair of
pants made by myself, from an old blanket once the property
of a lieutenant in the 22nd New York Reg't., who was shot
while leaning on my arm. My body was covered by an old
hospital gown that had been sent from the North by the Sanitary
Commission. The gown served as shirt, vest, and coat. A blanket
which I had secured extra served as a hat and military cloak.

BEHIND THE GUNS

We were visited in this camp by a number of prominent traitors among whom was [Brigadier] General [John H.] Winder, who was commander-in-chief of rebel prisons. He made us a speech in which he told us how sorry he was that he was unable to treat us no better, that his government was doing far better for us than their soldiers were receiving in Northern prisons. No wonder, the old traitor and liar died a few days later while abusing the poor starved creatures in one of the prison dens under his command. Another traitor who pretended to be very good, was a Dr. Palmer, a great D.D. of New Orleans. He frequently prayed for us — that is, for our souls — but he took good care to tell us that we could never subdue the South.

When the guns of Sherman's army were heard in Columbia, there was great excitement and hurry to get out of the city, and to take the prisoners along. We were put into box cars and held nearly all day. At dark our train moved out in the direction of Charlotte, N.C., while every prisoner who had a piece of hoopiron or an old jackknife, was hard at work making holes in the side of the cars and planning how to escape. When about half way between Columbia and Charlotte the train containing the Treasury of the so called Confederacy, running just ahead of us, jumped the track. Now was the time to take to the woods, but alas! it was raining and sleeting, cold and dismal as was the weather, and half naked as we were, we did not feel that we should be able to make a successful escape. The guards on top of the cars were nearly frozen. They climbed in beside us, saying, "If you'ens all want to go away, we'uns all can't help it"; and then they crawled in among us so that the animal heat might keep both friend and foe from freezing to death. The next morning we arrived at Charlotte, N.C., where we were encamped for a few days, and where the Union men of North Carolina showed us many favors.

Again I, with five others, escaped from the prison, and headed for the mountains where we struck the Catawba River in the night, near the little town of Morgantown. Lieutenant Oates of the 2nd Ohio cavalry and myself took the lead in crossing a long iron bridge, after first going up and down the river for miles, looking for a boat. When we were about half way across the others following instead of waiting to see the result of our crossing, we all walked right into the clutches of a rebel guard at the other end of the bridge. We were put into a little block-house and kept there till morning. When the news spread that

*there were Union prisoners in Morgantown, many came to see us,
and being mostly Union people they treated us very kindly,
bringing what they could spare us to eat. We were returned to
Charlotte, and in a few days after were sent to Goldsboro, N.C.,
where we were put into an enclosure near the railroad track
and exposed to the rain and storm for two days, when we were
loaded onto the cars, and this time were taken to Raleigh, N.C.,
where we were dumped out again near the railroad, surrounded
by high embankments. That night Captain Hays, of Sing Sing,
New York, and myself ran away and were off again, but did
not get very far. We paid a visit to Ex-Governor Holden in our
rags and dirt, then started for the wilderness, trying to meet
Schofield who we learned was marching up from Wilmington, but
upon meeting with a shoemaker who professed to be a Union man
we went with him to his house where he begged of us to stay
promising us to shelter us from the enemy, but the next morning
we were again in the hands of the rebels. I judged at the time the
fellow was playing us false and had sent for the provost-marshal.
We were taken back to the railroad embankment camp, and the
same night loaded onto flat cars this time, and taken to an old
conscript camp a few miles from Raleigh. At this point was made
the most diabolical attempt to take our lives of defenceless human
beings as was ever conceived by mortals.*

*The engine was pushing the train up the railroad, loaded with
at least a thousand human beings, when all at once it ran into
an open switch and nearly down a very high embankment
which, had we gone over, would have caused the death or
injury of every one on board, but the engine was not able to
get up steam enough to push the train over the embankment at
the end of the switch, and stuck fast, giving us time to jump off,
After remaining here a few days we were again loaded on the
cars and taken back to Goldsboro, where we were turned into
a pine woods, and here I saw the most intense suffering of my
whole life. It was a terrible sight to see the poor fellows who
had been sent here from other prison "hells," some of whom were
entirely without clothing, worn out with hunger and disease,
eaten with scurvy, teeth falling out, hair falling off. Oh horror!
and all this in a civilized country. Oh, how terrible is man's
inhumanity to man! The loyal people of Goldsboro went out
into the country and made collections of food for us, and did
the best that could be done to eleviate our suffering. After a
stay of three days we were again placed on the cars and sent to*

BEHIND THE GUNS

Magnolia, a village between Goldsboro and Wilmington, where on the eleventh of March, 1865, we were transferred to the United States forces, and then walked six miles into Wilmington.

When weighed I pulled down the scales at just ninety-six pounds. I was held a prisoner in rebel prisons just nine months and two days. After staying one day in Wilmington we were sent to Annapolis, Md., where I spent a few days in the hospital at the Naval Academy. The paymaster paid us here two hundred dollars each, and after getting some clothing we went to Washington, and there were paid off in full, and given thirty days furlough. On my return I joined the battery at Alexandria, Va., and received a very warm greeting from all the boys. This is a brief synopsis of what seemed to me a very long imprisonment.

I remain your old friend and comrade,
Charles McDonald,
Jr. 1st Lieut., Bat. I.
2nd Ill. Lt. Art.

PERSONNEL OF BATTERY I

CHARLES M. BARNETT of Joliet, Illinois, had been born in New York State and was twenty-four years old and unmarried when he enlisted for three years as a senior First Lieutenant on October 1, 1861, at Joliet. Barnett had earlier enlisted in McAllister's Battery (Co. K, 10th Infantry Regiment, three months service) on April 19, 1861 as a sergeant, later promoted to Lieutenant. He was mustered out on July 29, 1861, after serving in the "Expedition to Cairo."

He described himself as a clerk, 5 feet 8 inches in height, with light hair, blue eyes and a fair complexion. Barnett was mustered into service December 31, 1861, at Camp Butler. He was promoted to Captain sometime in late May or early June, 1862, but apparently not mustered in until sometime later. He was mustered in January 1, 1864, but this was a re-enlistment. His rank of Captain was to date from May 1, 1862; he resigned November 8, 1864.

JAMES R. BEDFORD of Joliet, Illinois, had been born in England and was seventeen years old when he enlisted for three years as a private on February 29, 1864, at Joliet; he was mustered at the same date and place. Bedford described himself as a farmer, 5 feet 6 inches in height, with brown hair, gray eyes and a light complexion. He was mustered out at Camp Butler, on June 14, 1865.

THOMAS BETTS of Aurora, Illinois had been born in the State of New York and was twenty-nine years of age when he enlisted for three years as a private on February 8, 1864, at Aurora. He was mustered into service

155

at Chicago on the same date. Betts described himself as a laborer, 5 feet 9 inches in height, with auburn hair, blue eyes and a dark complexion. He was mustered out June 14, 1865, at Camp Butler.

ALONZO W. COE of Joliet, Illinois, had been born in the State of New York and was twenty-nine years old and unmarried when he enlisted as a senior Second Lieutenant for three years on October 1, 1861, at Joliet. He had earlier enlisted in McAllister's Battery (Co. K, 10th Infantry Regiment, three months service) on April 19, 1861, as First Sergeant, and was mustered out on July 29, 1861, after serving in the "Expedition to Cairo." Coe described himself as being a farmer by occupation, 5 feet 11 inches in height, with dark hair, gray eyes and a fair complexion. He was mustered into service at Camp Butler, December 31, 1861. He was promoted to junior First Lieutenant, June 27, 1862 (to rank from April 7, 1862) and was killed in action near Savannah, Georgia, December 9, 1864.

PETER COUNTRYMAN of Plainfield, Illinois, had been born in the State of New York and was twenty-eight years old and unmarried when he enlisted as a corporal November 16, 1861, for three years, at Plainfield. He described himself as being a farmer by occupation, 5 feet 10 inches in height, with dark hair, gray eyes and a fair complexion. He was mustered into service at Camp Butler, December 31, 1861. He re-enlisted as a veteran on January 1, 1864, at Chattanooga, Tenn. as a private, and was mustered out June 14, 1865, at Camp Butler.

MARCUS D. L. COVERT, of Joliet, Illinois, had been born in Ohio and was twenty-six years old and unmarried when he enlisted as a corporal for three years on October 1, 1861, at Joliet. He described himself as being a boatman, 5 feet 5 inches in height, with black hair, brown eyes and a dark complexion. He was mustered into service at Camp Butler, December 31, 1861, and later deserted from the army.

ROGERS CUNNINGHAM of Peoria, Illinois, had been born in Ireland and was thirty-three years old and unmarried when he enlisted for three years as a private on November 25, 1861, at Peoria. He described himself as a laborer, 5 feet 9 inches in height, with dark hair, gray eyes and a fair complexion. Cunningham was mustered into service December 31, 1861, at Camp Butler. Nothing else is known of this man.

WARREN DIBIRT of Clinton, Illinois, had been born in Ohio and was nineteen years old and unmarried when he enlisted for three years as a private at Clinton on November 25, 1861. He described himself as a farmer, 5 feet 8 inches in height, with sandy hair, blue eyes and a light complexion. Dibirt was mustered into service at Camp Butler, on December 31, 1861. He re-enlisted as a veteran at Chattanooga, Tennessee on January 1, 1864, and was captured June 7, 1864, near Acworth, Georgia. He rejoined the Battery in Washington, D.C., in May, 1865. Dibirt was mustered out as a corporal at Camp Butler June 14, 1865.

THOMAS FINNELL of Clinton, Illinois, had been born in Ireland and was thirty-three years old and married when he enlisted for three years as a private on November 25, 1861, at Clinton. He described himself as a farmer, 5 feet 6 inches in height, with dark hair, gray eyes and a dark complexion. Finnell was mustered into service at Camp Butler, on December 31, 1861, and re-enlisted as a veteran at Chattanooga, Tenn., January 1, 1864. He was mustered out at Camp Butler June 14, 1865.

CHRISTIAN G. GEYER of Joliet, Illinois, had been born in Austria and was twenty-six years old and married when he enlisted for three years as a private on October 1, 1861, at Joliet. He described himself as a saddler, 5 feet 8 inches in height, with light hair, blue eyes and a light complexion. Geyer was mustered into service at Camp Butler, near Springfield, Ill., on December 31, 1861, and re-enlisted as a veteran at Chattanooga, Tenn., January 1, 1864, and died of wounds at that city September 18, 1864.

CHARLES D. HAIGHT of Naperville, Illinois, had been born in the State of New York and was forty-three years old and married when he enlisted as a quartermaster sergeant for three years on November 1, 1861, at Naperville. He described himself as a merchant, 5 feet 6½ inches in height, with sandy hair, black eyes and a fair complexion. He was mustered into service December 31, 1861, at Camp Butler, and promoted to Junior 2nd Lieutenant June 6, 1862; he was dismissed from the service March 1, 1863.

WILLIAM H. HAINES (or Haynes) of Kendall County, Illinois, had been born in Illinois and was twenty-one years old and unmarried when he

157

enlisted as a private for three years on October 1, 1861, at Joliet. He described himself as being a farmer, 5 feet 9 inches in height, with dark hair, gray eyes and a fair complexion. He was mustered into service at Camp Butler, December 31, 1861, and re-enlisted as a veteran at Chattanooga, Tenn., on January 1, 1864. Mustered out June 14, 1864 at Camp Butler.

WILLIAM EUGENE HAYWARD. Not much is known about Hayward because he was not with the battery when it was mustered. His rank as Junior Second Lieutenant dated from February 3, 1862. He was promoted to senior Second Lieutenant on April 7, 1862, and resigned February 2, 1863. Captain Barnett reported on February 10, 1863: "William E. Hayward, Sr. 2nd Lt. Batt. I, 2nd Ill. Arty, having been ordered before a 'Board of Examination' was found totally unqualified for the position that he had occupied for one year—and consequently was compelled to resign, which resignation was accepted February 2, 1863." Special Order No. 33, Headquarters, Dept. of the Cumberland, February 2, 1863, accepting Lt. Hayward's resignation, pointed out "Lt. Hayward is not a capable officer."

ROBERT HEATH of Channahon, Illinois, had been born in Illinois and was twenty-four years old and unmarried when he enlisted as a corporal for three years on October 1, 1861, at Channahon. He described himself as being a farmer, 5 feet 7 inches in height, with black hair and eyes and a fair complexion. He was mustered into service December 31, 1861, at Camp Butler. He re-enlisted as a veteran January 1, 1864, at Chattanooga, Tenn., and was mustered out at Camp Butler June 14, 1865.

HIRAM W. HILL of Aurora, Illinois, had been born in Scotland and was thirty years old and unmarried when he enlisted as a corporal for three years on October 25, 1861, at Aurora. He described himself as being a millright, 5 feet 9 inches in height, with dark hair, blue eyes and a fair complexion. He was mustered into service December 31, 1861, at Camp Butler, and re-enlisted as a veteran on January 1, 1864, at Chattanooga, Tenn. He was mustered out as a sergeant on June 14, 1865, at Camp Butler.

ALLEN B. HODGE of Decatur, Illinois, had been born in Illinois and was eighteen years old, when he enlisted for three years as a private on

December 29, 1861, at Decatur. He described himself as a farmer, 5 feet 10 inches in height, with dark hair, gray eyes and a fair complexion. He was mustered into the service after Battery I reached Nashville, Tennessee, but to date from December 29, 1861. He re-enlisted as a veteran at Chattanooga, Tenn., January 1, 1864, and was mustered out at Camp Butler, June 14, 1865.

ANDREW HOGAN of Chicago, Illinois, had been born in Ireland and was twenty-four years old and unmarried when he enlisted for three years as a private November 1, 1861, at Chicago. He described himself as a miller, 5 feet 8 inches in height, with light hair, blue eyes and a light complexion. He was mustered into service at Camp Butler, on December 31, 1861, and deserted on September 15, 1862, at Corinth, Mississippi, where he was serving a General Court Martial sentence.

CHARLES HOWARD of Peru, Illinois, had been born in Ohio and was twenty-six years old and married when he enlisted as a corporal for three years on November 1, 1861, at Chicago. He described himself as being an engineer, 5 feet 5 inches in height, with black hair, gray eyes and a fair complexion. He was mustered into service at Camp Butler, near Springfield, Illinois, December 31, 1861, and was mortally wounded at Island Number 10, March 17, 1862.

ISAAC W. JONES of Peoria, Illinois, had been born in Wales and was forty-eight years old and married when he enlisted for three years at Peoria as a private on November 25, 1861. He described himself as a miner, 5 feet 7½ inches in height, with brown hair, gray eyes and a light complexion. He was mustered into service at Camp Butler, on December 31, 1861, and was discharged for disability on September 10, 1864.

CHARLES W. KEITH of Joliet, Illinois, had been born in Rome, New York and was thirty-two years old and married when he enlisted as a captain in Joliet for three years on October 1, 1861. He described himself as being a banker, 5 feet 5 inches in height, with dark hair, grey eyes and a fair complexion. He was mustered into service December 31, 1861, at Camp Butler. He resigned on April 7, 1862.

JOHN A. KELLY of Joliet, Illinois, had been born in the State of New York and was twenty-four years old and unmarried when he enlisted as a first sergeant October 21, 1861, for three years, at Joliet. He described himself as being a physician, 5 feet 9 inches in height, with dark hair, blue eyes and a light complexion. He was mustered into service at Camp Butler, December 31, 1861. He resigned December 6, 1862, and enlisted in the 100th Illinois Infantry, where he was a First Lieutenant in Company K, and then promoted to Captain December 15, 1863. He was wounded both at Stones River and Missionary Ridge and was mustered out at Chicago on June 12, 1865, with the regiment.

LORENZO KELLY of Lockport, Illinois, had been born in the State of Pennsylvania and was twenty-seven years old when he enlisted for three years as a private on February 15, 1864, at Joliet. He described himself as being a cooper, 5 feet 6 inches in height, with brown hair, blue eyes and a dark complexion. Kelly was mustered in at Joliet, February 15, 1864, and was mustered out at Camp Butler on June 14, June 14, 1865, as a sergeant.

JOHN LINN of Chicago, Illinois, had been born in the State of New York and was twenty-three years old and unmarried when he enlisted for three years as a private on November 6, 1861 at Chicago. He described himself as a farmer, 5 feet 8 inches in height, with brown hair, blue eyes and a fair complexion. Linn was mustered into service at Camp Butler on December 31, 1861. He re-enlisted as a veteran at Chattanooga, Tenn., on January 1, 1864, and was mustered out at Camp Butler on June 14, 1865, as a sergeant.

WILLIAM MCALLISTER of Aurora, Illinois, had been born in Illinois, and was eighteen years old when he enlisted as a private for three years on February 15, 1864, at Aurora. He described himself as a farmer, 5 feet 10 inches in height, with light hair, blue eyes and a light complexion. McAllister was mustered into service at Chicago on February 29, 1864, and was later transferred to the invalid corps.

CHARLES MCDONALD of Peoria, Illinois, had been born in Scotland and was twenty-eight years old and unmarried when he enlisted as a private for three years on November 25, 1861 at Peoria. He described himself as being 5 feet 8 inches in height, with dark hair, blue eyes and a light complexion and an engineer by occupation. He was mustered into service at Camp Butler on December 31, 1861, and re-enlisted as a veteran January 1, 1864 at Chattanooga, Tennessee. McDonald was discharged as a First Sergeant February 29, 1864, and mustered in as Second Lieutenant March 1, 1864 (to rank from March 1, 1863). He was captured June 7, 1864, near Acworth, Georgia, and rejoined the Battery in Washington, D.C., in May, 1865, and was mustered out June 14, 1865 at Camp Butler.

GEORGE MATHER of Joliet, Illinois, was nineteen years old when he enlisted for three years as a private on January 1, 1862, at Joliet. He was mustered into service at Nashville, Tennessee, to date from January 1, 1862, and died from the effect of a scorpion bite on September 4, 1863, near Huntsville, Alabama.

JOHN M. MILLER of Mount Vernon, Illinois, had been born in Scotland and was thirty-four years old and married, when he enlisted for three years as a private at Mount Vernon, December 15, 1861. He described himself as a carpenter, 5 feet 8½ inches in height, with brown hair, black eyes and a dark complexion. Carpenter was mustered into service at Camp Butler, December 31, 1861, and he was injured in a railroad accident, arriving at a hospital at Indianapolis, Indiana, September 14, 1862, where he died of "concussion of the brain" on September 17, 1862.

ZACHARIAH MILLER of Joliet, Illinois, was born in Germany and was thirty-eight years old and unmarried when he enlisted for three years as a private, October 1, 1861, at Joliet. He described himself as a farmer, 5 feet 9 inches in height, with black hair, hazel eyes and a fair complexion. He was mustered into service at Camp Butler, on December 31, 1861. He re-enlisted as a veteran at Chattanooga, Tenn., and was mustered out at Camp Butler June 14, 1865, as a sergeant.

CHARLES P. MYERS of Joliet, Illinois, had been born in New Jersey and was eighteen years old and unmarried when he enlisted for three years as a private on December 18, 1861, at Joliet. He described himself as a laborer, 5 feet 6 inches in height, with dark hair, black eyes and a fair complexion. Myers was mustered into service at Camp Butler, on December 31, 1861, and he re-enlisted as a veteran at Chattanooga, Tenn., on January 1, 1864. He was mustered out at Camp Butler on June 14, 1865.

THOMAS PENNYWELL of Decatur, Illinois, had been born in the State of Indiana and was twenty-four years old and married when he enlisted for three years December 5, 1861, at Decatur. He described himself as a farmer, 5 feet 11 inches in height, with brown hair, gray eyes and a florid complexion. He was mustered into service at Camp Butler, on December 31, 1861, and re-enlisted as a veteran at Chattanooga, Tenn., January 1, 1864. He was finally discharged for disability.

MARSHALL PETERSON of Clinton, Illinois, had been born in the State of Ohio and was eighteen years old and unmarried when he enlisted for three years as a private on November 20, 1861 at Clinton. He described himself as a farmer, 5 feet 4 inches in height, with brown hair, black eyes, and a dark complexion. Peterson was mustered into the service at Camp Butler, on December 31, 1861, and re-enlisted as a veteran and bugler at Chattanooga, Tenn., on January 1, 1864. He was mustered out June 14, 1865, at Camp Butler.

HENRY B. PLANT of Peoria, Illinois, had been born in the State of New York and was thirty-one years old and unmarried when he enlisted as a Junior 1st Lieutenant for three years on November 9, 1861, at Camp Butler. He described himself as being a Curl Engineer, 5 feet 8 inches in height, with dark hair, blue eyes and a fair complexion. He was mustered into service at Camp Butler December 31, 1861; he was promoted to senior First Lieutenant April 7, 1862, and resigned because of disability May 6, 1864.

JUDSON RICH of Naperville, Illinois, had been born in the State of New York and was twenty-two years old and married when he enlisted as a sergeant for three years on October 25, 1861 at Naperville. He described himself as being a farmer, 5 feet 8 inches in height, with black hair and eyes, and a light complexion. He was mustered into service at Camp Butler, December 31, 1861, and promoted to senior Second Lieutenant March 24, 1863 (to rank from February 2, 1863); then to senior First Lieutenant May 6, 1864; and finally to Captain March 31, 1865 (to rank from November 8, 1864). He was mustered out June 14, 1865, at Camp Butler.

JOHN C. RILEY of Joliet, Illinois, had been born in Indiana, and was twenty years old and unmarried when he enlisted for three years as a private on December 17, 1861, at Joliet. He described himself as a laborer, 5 feet 6 inches in height, with dark hair, gray eyes and a fair complexion. Riley was mustered into service at Camp Butler, on December 31, 1861. He re-enlisted as a veteran at Chattanooga, Tennessee on January 1, 1864, and was mustered out at Camp Butler, on June 14, 1865.

EDWARD SMITH of Joliet, Illinois, had been born in Canada and was twenty-five years old when he enlisted for three years as a private on December 15, 1863, at Joliet. He was mustered into service at the same date and place. He described himself as a railroad man, 5 feet 10 inches in height, with black hair, gray eyes and a light complexion. Smith was mustered out as a Sergeant at Camp Butler, June 14, 1865.

RUFUS S. STOLP of Naperville, Illinois, had been born in the State of New York and was twenty-eight years old and unmarried when he enlisted as a sergeant for three years on Ocotber 25, 1861, at Naperville. He described himself as a carpenter, 5 feet 9 inches in height, with light hair, blue eyes and a light complexion. He was mustered into service December 31, 1861, at Camp Butler. He re-enlisted as a veteran January 1, 1864, at Chattanooga, Tenn. and was mustered out as a 1st Sergeant at Camp Butler, June 14, 1865.

GEORGE T. WARD of Naperville, Illinois, had been born in Illinois and was twenty-two years old and unmarried when he enlisted as a corporal for three years on October 25, 1861, at Naperville. He described himself as being a farmer, 5 feet 9 inches in height, with dark hair, brown eyes and a fair complexion. He was mustered into service at Camp Butler, December 31, 1861, and re-enlisted as a veteran January 1, 1864, at Chattanooga, Tennessee. He was promoted to senior Second Lieutenant May 6, 1864, but never mustered in as senior Second Lieutenant. He was discharged as First Sergeant March 30, 1865, and mustered in as junior First Lieutenant (to rank from December 9, 1864) on March 31, 1865. Lt. Ward was mustered out on June 14, 1865, at Camp Butler.

ABRAHAM WHITMAN of Joliet, Illinois, had been born in Canada and was twenty-five years old and unmarried when he enlisted as a sergeant for three years on October 1, 1861, at Joliet. He described himself as being a boatman, 5 feet 10 inches in height, with dark hair, gray eyes and a light complexion. He was mustered into service at Camp Butler, on December 31, 1869. No other information about Whitman is available.

A SONG OF BATTERY I

DEDICATED
TO
BATTERY I,
2ND ILLINOIS LIGHT ARTILLERY.

Its veterans in particular, by one of its recruits,
who enlisted at the time of its veteranizing.

J. R. Bedford, Verona, Illinois

TUNE.—*Marching through Georgia.*

No person who shall walk the earth, need ever feel ashamed
Of Battery I and what it did, not with it to be named;
But every heart may well feel proud (this truth can none gainsay,)
It did a noble part to save the Union.

Chorus   Hurrah! Hurrah! Our wish shall ever be,
That right prevail—our land be ever free—
Our flag, "Old Glory," still upheld, that all may in it see
The banner of the right and the Union.

To think of "Battery I's" career, and never to feel proud,
One's mind must be enveloped in the darkest kind of cloud;

For did it not do, first and last, good service through the war,
Ever upholding the Union.

Chorus

All hail, the battered bugle, boys, that sounded many a call!
All hail, the veteran comrades, who obeyed them, one and all!
Repented naught, braved everything, from first to last of war,
Ever maintaining the Union.

Chorus

From February, '64, 'till June of '65,
We served our Country with these brave old soldiers by our side;
They served from eighteen-sixty-one, and shared with us full praise
Of "Battery I's" most noble fight for Union

Chorus

When war began—this plea we make—we had not reached the age
That could endure a soldier's life, and Union cause engage,
Which cause immortalized each name of soldier, brave and true,
Which served through the war for the Union.

Chorus

Not one of us but wish, like them, that of us it were true;
That we'd been tried by every fight that Battery I'd been through,
And honors due them everywhere, o'er mountain and o'er lea;
We helped—but they it was, who saved the Union.

Chorus

How thankful we—our names are with these comrades old in war,
The roll of names some sixty then, (perhaps an odd five more;)
Now once a year we try to meet—there's left less than a score
Of those who manned the Battery for the Union.

Chorus

In times long passed, each day the roll was called and answered clear,
And prouder men ne'er stood in line than those who answered "here";
No hearts more sad with sorrow beat, when comrades "bit the dust,"
Than those who marched and fought to save the Union.

Chorus

"Assemblies" now are seldom, boys, not as in days of yore,
But, comrades, we shall meet again on that "brighter, better shore,"
Where Lincoln, Grant, and Sherman are, and all the "Loyal Blue,"
Who then stood bravely true for right and Union.

Chorus

INDEX

Ackworth, Georgia: Battery I camped near, 93

Adairsville, Georgia: C.S.A. works at Oostenaula River near, 90

Alexandria, Virginia: Battery I reaches, 139

Allatoona Pass, Georgia: C.S.A. positions at, 92; fight near, 116

Allatoona Station, Georgia: Battery I passes, 118

Alpine, Georgia, 117

Antelope, Steamer: transports Battery I, 12, 14

Army of the Cumberland: organized, 42 n.; mentioned, 43, 47

Army of the Mississippi, 9 n., 13, 14, 15

Army of the Ohio: composition of, 26 n.; Rosecrans commands, 41

Asboth, General Alexander S., U.S.A.: commands at Rienzi, 16; discontinues whiskey issue, 19

Athens, Alabama: Battery I reaches, 50, 51–52, 115; mentioned, 53

Atkins, Colonel Smith D., 120

Atlanta, Georgia: in sight, 100; Battery I fires on, 102; evacuated, 112; Battery I reaches, 113; destroyed, 120, 121

Atlanta Campaign, 87–113

Aurora, Illinois: ladies of present flag to Battery I, 80–81

Avers Ferry, North Carolina: Battery I reaches, 138

Baird, General Absolom, U.S.A., 120

Baldwin, Mississippi: Battery I reaches, 16

Bardstown, Kentucky, 27

Barnett, Charles M., of Battery I: concerned over shortage of men, xiii–xiv; recruiting, xv, xvi; Senior First Lieutenant, xii, 4, 6; commands detachment, 7; commands action at Island Number 10, 10; buries Howard, 11; assumes command of Battery I, 11, 11 n.; escorts prisoners to Cairo, 12; sent to Battery F, 15–16; leads advance, 16; reports Battery I to General Asboth, 16; in Hogan incident, 18; entertains friends, 19; commands Parrott guns at Perryville, 28, 36; visits Mammoth Cave, 41; appointed Chief of Artillery and Inspector of Horses at Nashville, 42; General Rosecrans compliments, 58; report of Battle of Chickamauga, 59 n.; reprimands driver, 60; under fire, 62; General Granger orders to fire, 64; trades cannons, 69–70; receives leave, 72; returns from leave, 76; precedes men to Springfield, 79; appointed Chief of Artillery, 2nd Division, xviii, 84; escapes ambush, 87; promotes Smith to sergeant, 96; directs fire, 106; complimented, 108 n.; acting Chief of Artillery, 14th Corps, 114; resigns, 117; career reviewed, 118; military biography, 155; mentioned, 26, 30, 46, 80, 84, 112, 128

"Barnett's Battery." *See* Battery I, 2nd Illinois Light Artillery

Beauregard, General Pierre G. T., C.S.A., 16

Bedford, James R., of Battery I: encounters dead soldier, 103; military biography, 155

Betts, Thomas, of Battery I: appointed acting quartermaster sergeant, 84–85; takes Sergeant Brown's place, 118; military biography, 155–56

Big Creek, Georgia, 126

Big Shanty, Georgia: Battery I moves toward, 94; mentioned, 113, 139

Blackjack Mountain, Georgia, 94

Blackland, Mississippi: Battery I in action at, 16

Blair, General Francis P., U.S.A., 103, 120

169

Shawnee Classics
A Series of Classic Regional Reprints for the Midwest